THE
NIGHT
OF
FEAR

Abha Sharma is a life coach, a freelance writer and a personality development trainer. She has worked extensively with international industry leaders in online education. A qualified university level educator, she has training in life sciences, English literature, journalism and creative writing, and has a deep interest in the mysteries of existence. She prefers to be identified as a student of life. With an immense faith in the human potential, she believes in unlearning for enhanced learning. As a life coach and a writer, it is her raison d'etre to help people find harmony within themselves.

Connect with her at:
LinkedIn: http://www.linkedin.com/in/abha-sharma-a1774a169/
Twitter: @abha_e

THE NIGHT OF FEAR

Abha Sharma

RUPA

Published by
Rupa Publications India Pvt. Ltd 2020
7/16, Ansari Road, Daryaganj
New Delhi 110002

Sales Centres:
Allahabad Bengaluru Chennai
Hyderabad Jaipur Kathmandu
Kolkata Mumbai

Copyright © Abha Sharma 2020

This is a work of fiction. Names, characters, places and incidents are either the product of the author's imagination or are used fictitiously and any resemblance to any actual person, living or dead, events or locales is entirely coincidental.

All rights reserved.
No part of this publication may be reproduced, transmitted, or stored in a retrieval system, in any form or by any means, electronic, mechanical, photocopying, recording or otherwise, without the prior permission of the publisher.

ISBN: 978-93-89967-60-9

First impression 2020

10 9 8 7 6 5 4 3 2 1

Printed at HT Media Ltd, Greater Noida

The moral right of the author has been asserted.

This book is sold subject to the condition that it shall not, by way of trade or otherwise, be lent, resold, hired out, or otherwise circulated, without the publisher's prior consent, in any form of binding or cover other than that in which it is published.

To

*My Dad, Romesh Dutt, who believed in me more than myself,
who is the reason I write, and whose life was a lesson in heroism,
for a hero emerges stronger after every challenge and never gives up.
I wish I could emulate even partly, his fighting spirit, his fantastic art of
storytelling, his skill with language, his understanding of human nature and the
infinite empathy of his heart.
And to my Mom, Madhurima, whose simplicity and optimism could instil hope
even in the most difficult circumstances.*

Contents

1. The 'Sinner' — 1
2. The Sun Should Rise in the West — 9
3. Trouble — 19
4. Danger — 29
5. Murder? — 39
6. The Monster — 45
7. Fear — 52
8. Disgust — 58
9. Woman — 64
10. The Curse — 69
11. Lonely — 76
12. Love? — 83
13. The Eyes — 89
14. Hope — 95
15. Warning! — 99
16. Unsafe! — 106
17. Lonely, But Not Alone — 113
18. The Truth — 119
19. The Challenge — 124
20. To the Temple — 130
21. Believers — 135
22. The Night — 141

I

The 'Sinner'

Victory Colony was a settlement of shacks and small houses situated in the valley just behind the Municipal Corporation buildings. A dirt road crawled like a snake into the locality. The settlement was inhabited mostly by migrant workers and their families who had come to this small Himalayan town for employment. The name of the locality had been carried on from colonial times when this part of the town served as a settlement for Indian policemen. Now, a few remnants of the old houses remained, their peeled-off walls displaying shades of dark yellow in the chunks of plaster that remained.

'Somewhere near the small shrine at the beginning of Victory Colony' was the address Pritha had gotten from the bakery owner. That is where Babulal, the victim of the temple lived. Pritha walked along the pavement hastily, ignoring the people who looked at her with surprise. Their reaction was understandable. They were not used to seeing a tall and slim, urban-looking nineteen-year-old undergraduate student dressed in jeans and a tank top in that area of the town. Pritha scanned the area till she spotted the small shrine. A couple of queries to the people standing there resulted in answers full of contempt for the 'sinner' and Pritha suspected, contempt for the person asking for him too. All the same, she was directed to Babulal's residence, but not before being pierced with warning looks.

Pritha followed the directions to reach a small house, with an old door and walls with visible cracks. She knocked. Someone unlatched the door from inside and opened it just a little.

'Who's there?' A young woman's frail voice asked.

'I am Pritha. Is this Babulal's residence?'

'What do you want?' The anxiety in the voice was unmistakable, almost offensive.

Pritha said soothingly, 'Nothing. I just want to see him. How is he doing? Can I talk for a couple of minutes?'

There was no reply. The woman inside latched the door again. Pritha stood there, unsure of what to do. She kept waiting for a few minutes and looked around. This part of the locality seemed exceptionally deserted, as if this house had been quarantined. She knocked again and waited. There was no reply, no sound.

Disappointed, she began walking away. A faint hope, though, made her stand and wait under a soap-nut tree opposite the house. Quite a few ripe, light-brown leathery berries lay on the ground. She picked up the one with a cracked shell and looked at the round black seed peeping from inside. The familiar, bitter smell of soap-nut was as far removed from sweetness as possible. Her eyes fell on a heap of similar black 'marbles', shoved in a crevice at the foot of the tree. *Kids' play! Poor children use these seeds in place of marbles, and what a game they play with these! We never told Ma that we used to play with these 'marbles' too, and that the gardener's children had taught us how to extract these from the berries.*

Pritha looked at the tiny house, more of a hut, and wondered why the children of that house had left this possession out in the open. Childhood memories goaded Pritha to pick up a few of those stony balls, to cup them in her hands and to hear the metallic sound of their rattle once again. She took the marbles in her hand and began tossing them, enjoying their clinking. Now and again, she glanced at the house, having a strange feeling that someone was watching her. Fifteen minutes must have passed when someone appeared at the window. It was a woman wearing a crumpled cotton saree, clutching the iron grill on the window with both hands. She looked sceptically at the girl standing under the tree, as if trying to judge her intentions. Pritha walked eagerly to the window.

'I mean no harm. Please, can I see Babulal?'

'He is unable to speak,' the woman said.

Pritha replied hastily, 'That's okay! I just feel concerned about what has happened to him.' The woman gave a startled look but remained silent. Pritha hesitated, wondering if she had said the right thing, and added, 'These marbles. Do they belong to your children?'

The woman bent forward to look at the black balls in Pritha's hand. Spontaneous tears rolled down her dry, brown cheeks. The woman peered deep into Pritha's eyes and turned away from the window. Pritha stood confused. In a few seconds, there was the sound of unlatching of the door. The door opened and the woman stood aside, waiting for Pritha to enter. The latter smiled hesitatingly at the woman and asked, 'Are you Babulal's wife?'

'Yes,' replied the woman, in a voice still laden with suspicion.

Pritha stepped inside the partially lit room and looked around at the unfortunate people's dwelling. Her eyes fell on a man lying on a cot. She froze in her steps. It was the man with curly hair; it was the shop assistant. He seemed to be in deep sleep. She gathered some courage and went closer. Pritha gasped in shock as she saw the man's face, twisted in a way she had never imagined was possible. His right hand lay on his chest in a crooked manner. He lay there with his eyes closed, like a helpless piece of wood.

Pritha swallowed air into her dry throat and exclaimed impatiently, as she turned towards the woman, 'Why is he at home? Why didn't you admit him to a hospital?'

The woman dragged a wooden stool and gestured to Pritha to

sit down. The latter was a little taken aback, but she sat down and looked at the woman. *Ignorance! These illiterate people suffer from ignorance.* The woman walked away to a corner of the room that was probably a makeshift kitchen, going by the few utensils that lay around. Pritha spoke with exasperation, 'In this condition, your husband needs medical care. He should be taken to a hospital. Why didn't you do that? I hope you do not believe in superstitious stuff?'

'Water?' The woman maintained a blank expression and held out a steel tumbler full of water in her hand. A surprised Pritha mumbled, 'No, thanks.' The woman turned away and placed the tumbler back on the floor and covered it with a bowl. Pritha felt a slight pang of guilt, as if she should have taken the water offered to her. The woman sat on the floor by the man's cot and started fanning him with a piece of cardboard. She started speaking in a heavy regional accent, alien to this town.

'They had dumped him on the road outside the colony...like a bag of garbage. He hadn't returned home that night. His phone was switched off. In the morning, I was told by neighbours that my husband had been thrown there by the temple people. They told me that he had been cursed...that he had committed a grave sin. I ran to him. He wasn't moving. People went by, but no one stopped. I cried for help. With folded hands, I requested people to help me take him to the hospital. No one came forward...they...they kept a distance...as if my husband was deadly infectious. Some shouted at me that a man who had angered the gods will not be taken in by any hospital.' The woman now looked at Pritha, intense pain shining through her yellowish eyes, and added, 'They had thrown him in the middle of the road... I somehow managed to pull and drag him to a corner of the street. I tried to give water to him... he did not drink. He was not speaking...he was not moving... but he was breathing.'

Pritha clasped her handbag tightly as she felt her throat

becoming drier. She looked at the moist eyes of the woman. The latter now looked at her husband, and continued in a voice wrapped in agony, 'I left him there; with my two little children sitting by him. I ran to the doctor's clinic nearby. I ran to the civil hospital. I pleaded with everyone I saw there…I pleaded with the doctors to let my husband be taken in. I asked them to at least come and check on him. One doctor agreed to come with me. While he was leaving the hospital, a group of people took him aside and told him something. He turned to me and refused to come.'

Tears freely flowed down Pritha's cheeks while the woman spoke without looking at her guest. 'The last time he spoke to me was when he was leaving his workplace. It was almost dark and he called me up to tell me that he would come home a little late as his employer had asked him to dispose of some worn-out idols. He said he was going to the mountaintop temple. We do not belong to this town. We had migrated from our village to this town only a month ago. We had no idea about the temple's rules. He said it was a good opportunity to see what the temple was like, so that someday he could take me and our children there…for an outing.'

At this, the woman broke down and cried without restraint, hiding her face in her hands. Pritha sat in silence, letting tears fall uninterrupted from her own eyes. A faint groan escaped the man's mouth. His wife sprung up from her seat and caressed his face. The man seemed to fall asleep once again. Pritha wiped her tears and patted her face dry with her hanky. She took a deep breath as she saw hope shining on the woman's face. A good couple of minutes went by but there was no other sound from the man. The woman sank back into her seat.

She mumbled, 'Never, ever, in our wildest imagination could we think of offending God. Why did we have to be the bearers of this sin?'

Pritha got up and walked to the woman. She placed her hand

on her shoulder and said softly, 'Your husband has not committed any sin. I know…'

The woman seemed to ignore what Pritha was trying to say and added in a half-thought, 'I sent my children to my sister's place. I feared for their lives. The people could do anything to them.'

Pritha was filled with disgust. Harming children? Even if this man would have been a criminal, how could anyone think of harming his children? She wanted to comfort the woman but struggled with words. A few minutes of silence went by and then Pritha managed to speak out, 'Please don't worry. I'll arrange medical care for him. I am just a student, but I'll do my best. How are you managing? Do you have enough money?'

'Whatever we had would be finished within a week.' The woman's voice was feeble now. Pritha promised to herself that she would do something about this. A fire was raging inside her now. She asked the woman if her husband had told her anything. Her hopes died when she was told that he had not spoken a word since the fateful night. Suddenly, the woman's face got clouded with suspicion. She asked hastily why Pritha had come there after all.

Pritha looked on, not sure what to say when the woman looked at her face and waved her hand, 'Ill fate has made me suspicious. Forgive me for that. You are still so young, but when you marry, you will come to know… I made a wedding vow to be with him forever… Whatever he will face, I will be a part of it. If I have to suffer for being with him, I'm ready.'

Pritha looked at the woman with unbounded admiration. Never in her life had she felt such immense respect for someone, respect that surged so strongly inside her that it seemed to have permeated the breath she was taking. She pressed the woman's hands warmly and looked at the man on the cot. She felt an urgent necessity to rush out and get help from somewhere. She comforted the woman, 'I'll try my best to get some help for you. I'll leave now.'

She turned and picked up her bag from the floor. All of a sudden, the woman grabbed Pritha's hand from behind. Startled, she turned back. The teary-eyed woman said, 'Ever since that cursed day, no one has spoken a kind word to us. You are the only one who came here and spoke to us like we were humans, not worms. You…have come as God's messenger to us. Can you please pray to God that He may forgive us? My husband committed a sin, but…he was ignorant.'

An overwhelming feeling of humility struck Pritha. She had never experienced this before, the vision of being a tiny dot on the unlimited canvas of this universe. Yet, two tiny dots were holding hands and a power radiated from that connection.

Pritha took heavy steps on the streets of Victory Colony, the woman's words and the events of that fateful evening rolling in front of her mental eyes. The sight of a sack-of-a-man lying on the temple floor, pleading with his attackers to let him go. The feeling of suffocation came back to her. *It is only me, only me in this entire world, besides the criminals, who know the truth. No one except me knows what happened at the temple on the mountain. It has been two weeks. Oh gosh! I have not been able to do anything about this. No one would believe me. The town is engulfed in wrong belief; my mother is engulfed in a wrong belief.*

Pritha retreated from the settlement with agitated steps. At the same time, she was not aware that her life-energy vibrated in a strange rhythm, making a subtle request to an unknown entity; a connection so subtle that it could not be apprehended through any known law of physics. She felt like a minuscule package of breath, yet intricately connected to the cycle of events. *This isn't just about me. This isn't just about the man.* Babulal's wife's words churned like a whirlpool inside her head: 'You have come as God's messenger to us. Can you please pray to Him that He may forgive us?' *Is a God really out there? Can a prayer save that man? How do*

I pray? Whom do I pray to? For the first time in her life, Pritha wished she had lent an ear to her mother's instructions about the methodology of praying.

She quickly invoked the logical faculties of her mind and began recalling the events of that day and the weeks after that. Those two weeks had been more than a lifetime for Pritha; her normal life had suddenly taken a plunge into a dangerous world. The way forward was becoming visible now, but she had to remember every detail, to figure out what to tell the superintendent of police. Would he too be of the other league? It would be dangerous if he was, but for now, telling him seemed to be the only option. There had to be a reason why she was becoming an instrument. It was an hour's walk to the superintendent of police's office and she decided to walk all the way to give herself time to recall everything.

2

The Sun Should Rise in the West

As Pritha walked towards the office of the superintendent of police, events from the past two weeks flooded her mind. It felt like another era…how her life had changed forever. She slowed her pace while passing by the display window of a large garment showroom and looked at the blurred image of her body among the mannequins. *How sure was I that I knew myself! A caterpillar too must be sure of who it is, till it starts turning into a butterfly. Metamorphosis must be a painful process!* She walked on and concentrated her thoughts on that day when it all began.

∽

'Come home on time today if you want us to stay out of danger' read the text message on Pritha's cell phone. Pritha held the phone under the desk, glanced at the time display and put the phone back on her lap. She picked up her pen and resumed looking at the chalkboard while the botany professor explained a floral diagram to an undergraduate class of around forty students. She heard the professor's voice, which at that moment seemed to be mere sound floating in the air without meaning. Pritha considered the idea of sending a reply of disagreement to her mother's message. That would be easy. The hard part would be making her mother, Beena, see the truth. Even though Pritha was only nineteen, she could understand that like the rest of this Himalayan town, her mother had consciously chosen fear over freedom.

Pritha looked blankly at the chalkboard. The diagram, a circular shape with conical edges, appeared incomprehensible. She took her pen and tried to copy the diagram. In about a minute, the diagram in her notebook was a messy mixture of semi-circles, cones and crisscross lines drawn so strongly at places that the page was partially torn. A while later, she stopped abruptly and turned to a blank page and began staring at it.

Her mother had been repetitive in the last few days, repetitive to the extent of becoming obsessed. As much as she loved her mother, she hated the idea of giving in to this unreasonable demand. This morning too, Beena had shouted after Pritha as the latter was leaving home for college, 'Don't forget to come back on time, Pritha. Else…' Pritha had turned back and made a reassuring gesture to her mother standing in the doorway, though she had wanted to shout back a 'no'. Her thoughts returned to the classroom. She tried to reason out with herself. *All right. Fine. This is the last time I'm complying. After this, I'll do everything to convince Mom to free herself of this stuff.*

Pritha looked around at her friend Mili sitting two rows away from her, hoping that the latter would look back and she could silently share her discomfort. She saw Mili staring blankly at her desk, deep in thought. An alarmed Pritha bent forward, wanting to see her friend's expression, when for some reason, the professor suddenly announced in a loud, authoritative voice, 'The sun always rises in the east'. Pritha narrowed her eyes at the professor and started thinking. *O sun, for once, please rise in the west. Just for a day, I want to see you there! Just for a day, somebody please reverse the spin of this planet!* The rebellion in the thought refreshed Pritha; it amused her. It gave her a feeling of semi-revenge, though she did not know who the revenge was against, her mother's recent whims, or the arrogance in the professor's voice. She folded her arms, sat back in her chair, smiled, and looked at the professor like an enigmatic, mischievous kingmaker.

The professor mentioned some other airy concepts that Pritha did not hear because she was enjoying the spectacle playing in her mind of the sun shining in the northern sky. *How funny every professor will look when that happens! What will they do with their extreme pride of 'knowing things'? One day, the moon should rise in the morning, to teach these sticklers a lesson.* Pritha lowered her head to hide the smile that had brightened up her face.

The bell rang and the lecture ended. Just as everybody got up to leave the room, Pritha's eyes searched for Mili. She saw the latter still sitting on her seat. Pritha sprang up, tucked her notebook, phone and pen into her bag, grabbed it and made her way around the desks, her slim body easily negotiating the spaces between the desks. She touched Mili's arm, concerned about the shadows that hung about her friend's countenance.

'Are you okay, Mil?'

Mili gave a small nod. Pritha blurted out in a voice laced with annoyance, 'What is he up to now?'

Mili shot a sharp look at her friend but then controlled herself and whispered, 'I need to talk to you, Pritha.'

'Of course! Let's go to the garden,' Pritha said and the two walked out into the corridor, ignoring the group of ever-inquisitive girls at the doorway, always ready to locate a sad expression on somebody's face and to weave a whole story around it, complete with a moral.

'Oho! Where to, Queen of Jhansi?' one of the girls shouted after Pritha. The latter restrained herself from responding. She took that 'title' more as an offence rather than a compliment. She hated the sarcasm in the title. It singled her out from the crowd of people who were indifferent to things around them. In the short period since she had joined this college, Pritha had become quite visible in the college circles, having had strong arguments with the management over underage helpers and about the lack of facilities for the support staff. All that would have gone down well with her classmates had she not lectured them about the need to be more concerned about social issues. So, she was termed 'Mahatma Gandhi', 'Queen of Jhansi' and the perceived equivalents.

In the crowded corridor, Pritha looked at her friend walking beside her, wondering why she would have to go for a needless excursion with her mother the day her closest friend needed her the most. She thought it would be better to tell Mili about the time constraint. As the two made their way through groups of students, Pritha said, 'Mili, I'll have to leave early today. Mom is adamant that she will take me to that mountaintop temple today. It is some full-moon-day belief.' Exasperation from Pritha's thoughts percolated into her words and she added, 'Why does Mom have to believe in weird stuff like the whole town? She is better educated!'

Mili replied, 'Maybe she feels good there. Maybe that place will do some good to you too, Pritha. I've been there many times and I felt good.'

Pritha gave a sarcasm-laden look to her friend. 'Oh, come now, Mili! Don't get so meek and scared because people tell strange stories about that temple! I suspect that place inspires fear more than reverence among the people of this town.'

The town was like a polished stone embedded in the hills of the Shivalik ranges. At first look, it appeared to be a small, remote, hill town rich with nature's beauty…just that. Non-natives had little idea that this place had kept pace with every modern development and the townspeople prided themselves at having every facility that would be available in a cosmopolitan city. The spirit of the town had remained the same for decades, though.

Pritha led Mili out of the corridor into a small garden. The college had been built on four different levels on a hillside. There was hardly any stretch of land at a continuous level in this town, so larger structures were usually constructed upon several tiers by carving out slopes. The science block was at the lowest level and had the luxury of a reasonably sized garden outside it. The garden was usually quiet at that time of the day. Pritha scanned the area and spotted just two students standing in the far corner. She pulled Mili by the hand to a concrete bench in another corner of the lawn. By this time, Mili's face was covered with a steady flow of tears.

'What has he done now?' It was more of a rebuke rather than a question from Pritha.

Mili just sobbed. Pritha shook her head in disapproval. Mili sobbed louder and rested her head on Pritha's shoulder. Pritha, however, was in no mood for sympathy. She held her friend by the shoulders and shook her mildly.

'How many times have I told you to get rid of that rotten selfo!'

'Selfo' was their unique term for selfish people. Pritha and Mili had been friends since their pre-school days and they had a whole list of secret terminologies between them. Mili continued sobbing.

'What's the matter?' Pritha got impatient. She waited for a minute, and then added, 'Will you tell me something or do you want to dehydrate yourself with these tears?'

Mili gave her sobs a pause. Without saying anything, she opened a text message on her phone and gave the phone to Pritha. It read; 'Ill tk a weeks time to decide.'

'Can't he even write in full spelling? And what is this? HE will take a week! Kick off that asso, that so-called boyfriend, right now! You do it!'

While Pritha was busy with her outburst, Mili took out a tissue from her bag, sprinkled water from the bottle she carried and wiped her face. Patting another dry tissue on her cheeks, Mili said, 'You don't understand, Pritha. I really like him.'

'I've known you since ages, Mili. You don't like him. You have only gotten used to him being around. Can't you see that he has been using you as a temporary accessory?'

'You are wrong. I'm sure Pankaj loves me. He only needs time.'

'You don't love someone so badly at nineteen years that you decide to spend the rest of your eighty-one years with him.' Pritha paused, wondering at her own statement. Eighty-one years would be a long time to live. What would she do with so much of time?

Mili looked at Pritha and spoke in a louder voice, 'If he didn't love me, he wouldn't have fought with those boys over me that day. He has also been giving me gifts and those cost him something. And what is more important is that we have discovered we are quite similar!'

Pritha took a long breath and made an attempt to have Mili revisit her memory. 'You keep forgetting, Mili, that he proposed to you only to win a bet, a bet he had placed with his friends. Don't you remember how hurt you were when you found this out?' Pritha tried to be more logical rather than angry now. 'Now that he has proven his point, that he can have a girlfriend, and she would be his girlfriend for some time, he wants to end this. Can't you see?'

'It is not that simple, Pritha. It's true he had done this to win a bet. He had said sorry to me and I had forgiven him. It is different now. Maybe he is feeling guilty, that's why he wants to end it. Since I have now come to care for him, I can't leave him like that. It is in moments like these that true love is tested.' Mili tried to deepen her voice to sound convincing.

Pritha shrugged and spent the next few minutes trying to reason with Mili that it was more than obvious that Pankaj was not interested in a serious relationship with her. She mentioned recent instances to remind Mili how this guy had been finding excuses to break off by deliberately hurting her. Mili, on the other hand, thought more with emotion than reason. In her mind, she lived in a world of Hindi movies where love could come floating on a whiff of air, enrapturing two mortals with its magic and binding them in an invisible bond that the world could never understand.

For about half an hour, Pritha worked hard to make Mili see reason. But then, she abruptly stopped. She noticed an unfamiliar expression on Mili's face. The latter appeared to be getting visibly uncomfortable with what Pritha was saying. Pritha looked deep into Mili's eyes. It was something more than discomfort…it was dislike! She gaped at her friend's face, desperately trying to translate that look. Numerous times the two girls had disagreed and argued and fought and had patched up. But this reaction was unfamiliar, it gave Pritha the feeling of suddenly stepping out into the adult world, where they were two different women, not 'friends'.

Mili gave Pritha a purposeful look, a frown outlining the displeasure in her eyes. And then, she put her thoughts into words.

'You won't understand, Pritha.'

Pritha stared at Mili with a questioning look.

'Pritha, I know that you are tall and fair and slim, that you have a great figure and that you have nice skin and hair… But the fact is that…that you have never had a boyfriend. Never. Do you see, I am short, my hair doesn't shine like yours and I don't have a great face? I am a little overweight. But…I have a boyfriend.'

The words shot into Pritha like a million arrows that injected painful poison into every nerve in her being. She gazed at Mili as if she had neither speech nor sight. The person she was looking at was not the childhood friend she knew better than she knew herself. It was some other young woman. It was some other person whose eyes screamed, 'You don't like the fact that I have achieved more than you by having a boyfriend'.

Pritha sat glued to her seat. After a few minutes of lifeless silence, she got up clumsily and tried to grab her bag from the bench but missed. She reached out again with her shaking hands, gripped the bag and trudged towards the main gate of the college.

Mili did not make any effort to stop her.

Shock flooded Pritha's mind and froze all thoughts. She could see things and people, but could not think of them in words. She started the thirty-minute walk to her home with quick steps, almost tumbling over at a speed breaker on the road. The warm afternoon air blew into her face. In a few seconds, her vision got blurred. The shock had started melting into tears and the latter slid down her cheeks. The tears, however, helped ease the rocky heaviness of her mind and set her thinking again.

Thoughts stormed through her mind as she walked along a busy road. Through all their teenage tribulations, Mili had become Pritha's emotional treasurer. All these years of growing up had been a time of carefree sharing with Mili; sharing of her darkest thoughts, her deepest desires and her unabashed feelings about sensitive topics. Pritha had never given a thought as to how Mili would interpret any of these secrets. She had never judged Mili because Mili had always been there in her life, like her arms or her legs. In one stroke, something had snapped between these close friends. A pang of stingy pain struck Pritha. She felt vulnerable, as if her reflection in the mirror had suddenly become judgmental.

The pain grew with the realization that Mili had perhaps never understood the true intent of her words. *Perhaps she had never been aware of the real me.* Mili, after all, was too much like everyone else. She was like Pritha's mother, who would never understand her. Agony came ashore during such moments, moments when Pritha wondered whether there was anyone out there who could appreciate her for thinking differently.

She hadn't realized how quickly her thoughts brought her closer to her home. She had to face a different scenario here; going to the temple with her mother. Her uneasiness grew as she recollected how her mother was getting increasingly obsessed with that strange place and its priests. As if that was not enough, Beena had been making persistent efforts to convince her family to accompany her to the temple. Pritha's father, Brij, a businessman, was a busy person. He got busier at the mention of such excursions. Pritha, the only child of the couple, had successfully evaded the topic till now, but this time, Beena was adamant that she would take Pritha with her. Only, they must come back from the temple before it got dark. No one ever dared to stay up there after sundown.

If she could, Pritha would have locked herself in her room the whole evening, sunk into her bed, and would have tried to figure out the reason for Mili's sudden and unexpected acrimony. She would have to wait till nightfall for that opportunity. She wiped her face to remove any traces of tears and rang the doorbell, hoping that her mother would not notice her moist eyes. Beena opened the door and without looking at her daughter closely, passed on quick instructions.

'Pritha, I have kept a dress ready for you. It's there on your bed. Come, get ready quickly, have your lunch and let's go soon after that.'

Pritha did not make any attempt to start a conversation with her mother and went straight to her room. She saw a black embroidered kurta, red leggings and a red stole on the bed. That traditional ensemble was very different from the tee-shirt–jeans–skirt outfits she usually wore.

Pritha freshened up and got dressed. As a matter of habit, she switched on the lights in her room and stood looking at the mirror. The artificial lights couldn't cause any noticeable change in the room illuminated with daylight. She looked at the wall lights. *The heroes and the heroines of the night; the insignificant creatures of the day, let me switch you off.* She turned off the lights and looked at her reflection again. She brought her hand to the broad neckline of her black shirt and stepped closer to the mirror. In a rush of spontaneity, she rolled in the margins of the neckline, revealing the smooth skin of her shoulders and chest. With a gentle stroke of her hands, she gathered her long, silken black hair in a cluster and rolled them to one side, resisting a sudden urge to apply bright lip colour and to put a little kohl to her eyes.

'You have never had a boyfriend, Pritha.'

I don't need a damn boyfriend! I won't have a boyfriend just for the sake of having one!

Pritha's mother knocked at the door to remind her that they needed to hurry up. 'I'll take just a minute more, Ma,' Pritha called out and straightened out the neckline of her shirt.

3

Trouble

The temple, a white-coloured structure, stood atop a mountain in the western part of the town. Wild vegetation covered a major part of this mountain, with pine trees standing tall among a mass of undergrowth. Its lower parts, however, were dotted with a few small houses built on small areas of land on the gentle slopes. Pritha walked beside her mother on the narrow road that crept up to the temple. The previous night's rain had washed the dust off every plant and the green leaves looked irradiated on the warm, clear August afternoon.

Pritha hadn't noticed the brightness of the surroundings earlier. Now, when she did, it made her uncomfortable; it was so antagonistic to her state of mind. She constantly brushed aside the urge to check her phone for messages, trying to convince herself that she didn't care whether Mili wanted to contact her or not. Yet, she glanced at her phone now and then, almost wishing there was a message from Mili. There was none. She finally shoved the phone into her sling bag and looked at her mother. The latter's pace had slackened. The slope was steep and Beena carried seventy-five kilos in her body at around fifty years of age. The distance to the top was around one and a half kilometres. They were only halfway up and Beena was already breathing heavily.

'Let's stop for a few moments, Ma. You are tired.'

'Are you crazy? We cannot afford to be late,' Beena snapped.

Pritha knew it was no use insisting, just as it had been no use trying to put sense into Mili's head. Pritha thought deeply. There was fear in her mother's voice and she knew the cause of this fear—the legend. This Himalayan town woke up, lived and slept in the belief of this legend. It was rumoured that any ordinary person who dared to venture into the main shrine of the temple after dusk, was doomed to a horrible fate, even death. For years, this story had been circulating among the people of this town.

The legend was woven around an incident that happened about fifty years ago, on the evening when the idol was placed in the temple, marking the construction of the temple as complete. On that fateful day, as soon as the sun had set, dark clouds started gathering in the sky. Soon, there was a thunderstorm and heavy rains poured down. A middle-aged villager who had been travelling on foot, took shelter inside the shrine, and stayed there the whole night. He was found dead in the morning. Some people said he was bitten by a snake; others said he had been suffering from a fatal ailment. Most people said he was a healthy man and it must have been some mysterious force that ended his life. There were many assumptions, but credence was given only to the words of the then presiding priest of the temple, also the founder of the temple organization. He was known as the 'Mahaguru' or the great guru.

It was said that the day following the incident, the Mahaguru had announced he had been illuminated with extraordinary knowledge and that a revelation had come to him in the form of a dream. He had dreamt that the temple was a rare pure spot on Earth, a divine blessing for the people of this town. However, he cautioned that common people should approach such a sacred place carefully. They must not enter the temple after dark, because it was the impure time of the day when dark forces could take control of any mortal. If such a person affected with the devilish forces entered the shrine, the temple would be defiled and the deity would be enraged.

Thus, only the priests who had been 'initiated' could enter the shrine after dark. Such priests were given special training that remained a closely guarded secret inside the organization founded by the Mahaguru. It was said that these priests had been purified in a manner that no dark forces could touch them, hence only they could visit the shrine after dusk. For those who were initially sceptical, another recent incident put the seal of truth to this legend. Around fifteen years ago, a twelve-year-old boy had ventured into the shrine at night for unknown reasons and his lifeless body was discovered the next morning. His parents had accepted his death as the will of the deity and had not pursued the matter.

Pritha glanced at her mobile phone. It was half past three in the afternoon. Their visit should be over well before dusk. She looked up towards the top of the mountain and wondered what the place would feel like. She had never given serious thought to how much she believed in the divine, or if she believed at all. Her young mind had been too occupied with other things. That day, her mind was saturated with painful disbelief. *Could a friendship snap just like that? Could there be something called fate and stuff? Why did this happen? Will I find some solace in the temple? Can I get my answers there, as other people do? Nah! All those 'I went there...my life changed' narrations are so stale! Religious stuff is so unlike life. Okay, fine! If Mili wants to live without me, I'm okay with that. I can survive without her...! At least it is better than being misunderstood by the person you trust the most...*

'We shouldn't be late.' Beena's loud assertion brought Pritha's attention back to her mother. To get respite from her mother's obsessive urgency, Pritha looked around and noticed the rich vegetation on both sides of the road—yellow buttercups, red salvia and white aster flowers among the wild herbs and bushes of all sizes. Five minutes later and up closer to the temple, the natural vegetation soon gave way to trimmed hedges and concrete flooring. The entrance to the temple complex was an open one, without a gate. Two concrete pillars on either side supported an arc on the top. Two young men in kurta-pajamas were standing at either side of the entrance, sprinkling water at the people who were entering the temple premises. This was supposed to be a ritual of purification that was done to prevent any impure thing or person from entering. A concrete pavement flanked by rose hedges led to the main shrine. Dozens of people moved around the temple complex. Beena said to Pritha with pride, 'See, I told you. The entire town comes here on a full moon day.'

'Ma, this night is going to be a full moon night. Then what's the connection with the day? Why a full moon "day"?'

Pritha saw her mother getting flustered with the teasing. Beena raised her eyebrows but chose not to reply. In less than a minute, the two stepped inside the temple. Pritha wasn't surprised at how little she remembered from her last visit many years ago. The hall, with a high ceiling, was larger than she had thought. Huge windows with clear glass panes lined the two sides of the hall. The statue of the deity was positioned on the far end of the hall, on a pedestal under a colourful concrete canopy. It was difficult to tell the form of the statue as it was covered to the top in garlands. The fragrance of incense announced that this was a different domain. Pritha joined the queue with her mother. As the line moved ahead slowly, she looked out through the windows. The view to her right caught her attention. There was a garden with a rich collection of flowering plants but unlike the other parts of the temple complex, there was no one moving around here. Perhaps it was a restricted area, Pritha thought. If they would allow students there, this place could be a treasure house for her herbarium project.

After about fifteen minutes of inching ahead, they finally came closer to the pedestal. Two priests guarded the barrier that had been installed to disallow anyone to go close to the statue of the deity. One of the priests took the offerings from Beena and mechanically tossed them on to a table at the feet of the idol. In return, he dumped prasad on to her hands and then on to Pritha's. He gestured with his hands that they should move ahead. Pritha looked on in surprise, finding it difficult to believe that this was the only thing they came here for. She looked around. People seemed to be quite used to this quick, indirect meeting with the deity.

'That's it, Ma?' Pritha asked her mother.

Beena whispered, 'Nothing much to do here, but we'll have to spend some time in the adjoining hall. The head priest lectures there.'

Pritha looked on at her mother in confusion. *This is the temple, isn't it?* However, this was not the place for an argument, so without saying anything, she followed Beena to another room connected by a doorway. It was a large room with a small rectangular stage on which the head priest of the temple was sitting. At least a hundred people sat on the durries laid down on the floor. As men and women entered the room, they bowed before the priest before taking a seat on the durries.

Pritha's mother folded her hands in respectful greeting to the priest and signalled to Pritha to sit down. Pritha's attention, though, was diverted by the vibration of her phone in her sling bag. She silently pointed to her bag and exited the room while her mother sat there with enraged disagreement written clearly on her face. Pritha quickly stepped out into the verandah and received the call. It was Vandana, a common acquaintance of Mili and Pritha.

'Hey Pritha, is everything okay?'

Pritha answered in confusion, 'Yes, but why this question?'

'Nah, nothing as such, I just saw Mili leaving the college alone. Both of you usually leave together, no? You were not there in the last two classes too. Mili had something unusual about her. I just thought I'll enquire if all is well.' Vandana tried to sound casual.

Pritha sensed waves of displeasure rising within her. She had no patience with nosey people whose favourite game was to pose as if they were the most caring people on this planet. Vandana was endowed with such quality and this forced Pritha to avoid her company as much as possible.

Pritha replied with assertion, making no effort to hide the irritation in her voice, 'Everything is okay, Vandana. Right now, I am busy. I'm out somewhere with my mom. Talk to you later.' She disconnected the call.

Back inside the lecture hall, she sat next to her mother and suffered the latter's annoyance-ridden glances. She was about to whisper something to pacify her mother when her phone rang one more time. It was Vandana calling again. Pritha declined the call, put her phone on silent mode and avoided looking at Beena this time. Instead, she looked ahead at the priest giving the lecture, trying her best not to utter an abusive word for Vandana.

∽

It was ten in the night and Pritha sat at the edge of her bed, looking down at the floor. Her parents had retired to their room and the house was quiet. Her phone, lying beside her on the bed, rang. Pritha grabbed the phone, saw Vandana's name flashing on the screen, declined the call and switched off the device. This was the third time that Vandana had tried to call her since the evening but Pritha had declined each of the calls. She got up, opened the drawer of her study table and put her phone inside it. She started pacing around the room, trying to solve the muddle in her head. Mili still hadn't made any attempt to contact her. *Perhaps the friendship was...over*. 'Over' seemed to be an unbelievably strong word. It pierced Pritha. Does that mean all her life's sharing with Mili had been like flushing her precious diamonds down the sink?

This sounded painful. Spirals of recollections rose in Pritha's mind. She took a sip of water from the tumbler on her study table and sat down on the chair. She leaned back and looked out of the large window by the table.

The full moon, a perfect circle, was up in the night sky. On such nights, Pritha had often had an irresistible desire to sneak out of her room to her secret heaven. Her house was flanked at the back by part of a hill slope. In that town, it was common to have part of a hill in the backyard or on the side of the house. This patch of the hill, around one thousand square metres in area, was special. It had retained its wilderness. It was covered with green mountain grass dotted at places by wild globe thistles, yellow dandelions and raspberry plants. There were a good number of old pine trees flanked by fragile baby pines. This land was somebody's disputed property on which no human mark had been etched other than an irregular barbed-wire fence that surrounded the patch of greenery. For Pritha, it had been a secret sneak-out for many years. On clear summer nights, she would often cross the barbed-wire fence that just touched the boundary wall of her backyard. She would walk around a dozen steps from her home and sit near her favourite rock. This spot was perfect, just a few steps away from her home but a good distance away from the other houses.

Pritha opened the rear door of the house, taking care not to make any sound, and latched it from outside. As she did so, she imagined what her parents would think of her excursion. Her mother would be hysterical at the thought of her girl going out of the house alone at night on a mountain slope! Her father would give her a grave look and would ban her outings to the wilderness. However, no one had ever discovered this and perhaps never would. Pritha climbed up the gentle slope. Pine needles formed a slippery carpet, but she was habituated to walking on it. She brushed the small clearing at the base of the rock with her hand and sat down with her back against the rock. She looked up at the moon. The moon looked at her.

How quietly the moon rises, like a shy celebrity, it peeks out from behind the hill and does not show up till all have settled in their homes. And when darkness envelops everything, towns and villages are hushed, birds have slept in the trees and quietness rules, the moon comes out and glides past the night sky.

When the sun rises, it is determined to send its bright light into every possible crevice of this world, waking up people from their sleep, leading to the clatter and clinking of worldly living. Oh! My mind already hears the clatter of a shattered friendship.

Pritha looked at the moon more intently. Her silent conversations with the moon had given peace to her mind innumerable times. Perhaps, the moon understood her, unlike the people in her life. She looked at the moon without blinking, aware that in a few moments, the magic would begin. She saw the perfect circle with imperfect shapes in it. Gradually, the moon gained a halo. Now, it was the only thing that existed in the sky; all else had temporarily faded. Pritha inwardly shivered with a pang of pleasure at feeling herself so close to the king of the night sky. The beauty of the moon's serene face enraptured her. She felt her mind freeing itself from her body and becoming one with the silky moonlight. They were entwining; she was being drawn, almost as if she was melting to become one with the moon. She lost control of her body; the charm of the full moon was working.

Like the gentle blossoming of a bud, Pritha opened her being to receive calm signals. It was the magic of a soft conversation between a mind and a celestial entity. She smiled even more, bathing her soul in the bliss. Minutes passed, perhaps an hour passed; time did not matter. This could go on for eternity. The moon, however, kept tab of time. After numerous such blissful moments, it turned playful and covered itself up with the branch of a pine tree. Pritha came out of her trance. She had to get up now. She stood up and narrowed her eyes at the moon.

Lovely Moon behind the pine leaves,
You make me mad.
I've watched you watching me often,
And saying nothing.

⁂

It was eight in the morning when Pritha opened her eyes softly. The jangling of utensils from the kitchen and the sound of her mother's voice directing the housemaid woke her up completely. She turned around in her bed, wanting to sleep more. She reluctantly glanced at the wall clock and then sat up on the bed with a jerk. She had overslept and could get late for college unless she hurried. She opened the drawer of her table and switched on her phone. She raised an eyebrow when she spotted a text message from Vandana. After a brief initial reluctance, she opened the message. It read: 'Need to talk to you urgently'.

What the…! Why is she after me? I'll call her right now and tell her upfront that she should stop poking her nose into my affairs that she has no right to interfere in.

Pritha quickly dialled Vandana's number. As soon as the latter received the call, she said in an urgency-laden voice, 'Oh Pritha, I've been trying to talk to you since last evening. Do you know that thing about Mili?'

'What thing?' Pritha said in an emotionless voice.

'That thing about Mili and her boyfriend? Wait, you don't know about it? Just as I guessed; Mili has kept it a secret from you too.'

'What thing, Vandana? Stop this guessing game and if it is worth anything, tell me about it. And do keep in mind: Don't comment on my friendship with Mili.'

'Come on, Pritha! Why would I comment upon your friendship? This is something serious. I think Mili is in trouble. But I can't tell this to you over the phone. Let's meet in college ASAP.'

Pritha sensed that it was not the usual, prying Vandana. There was something else. She agreed to meet her in the college canteen before the classes would begin and hung up the call.

Pritha's first instinct was to call Mili. She fiddled with the phone in her hand. *No, I won't call. It is not some stupid ego. It is self-respect!*

She tried to calm herself down, but her mind had already started spinning out chaotic thoughts. She got ready and rushed to the dining table. Her parents were sitting on the table, waiting for Pritha to join them for breakfast. Beena was describing the previous day's excursion to her husband, explaining with great passion how 'blissful' and 'soothing' she felt after that visit. Pritha looked at her father, who was applying butter on his toast with great concentration. He was always disinterested in such talk but was always a patient listener. Pritha gulped down her breakfast and rushed to college.

4

Danger

Pritha and Vandana sat across a table in a dimly lit corner of the college canteen. The lack of bright light in that spot created an illusion of secrecy. There weren't many people who could overhear them, though. Only three other students sat in the far corner, engrossed in their discussion. Pritha took a few eager sips of soft drink from the bottle in her hand to ease the dryness in her throat. She looked at Vandana, who ran her fingers around the can of diet soda she had ordered, waiting for a question from Pritha. The latter detested this 'give-me-importance' attitude of her 'kind-of-a-friend' but began the conversation anyway.

'Look, Vandana, if you want to enquire about my friendship with Mili…'

Vandana cut her short, 'Why would I ask anything about it? You two are best friends. As a common friend who means well, I was curious whether you are aware of the trouble Mili is putting herself into. And it is clear that you don't know about it. She must be crazy not to take you into confidence.'

'What kind of trouble? What is it?' Pritha asked impatiently.

She could see that hint of a sneer on Vandana's face. On earlier occasions, Pritha had secretly observed Vandana's habit of smiling at other people's misfortunes. She would have kept a lifetime of distance from this girl had they not been obliged to interact often, being part of the same class and the same laboratory activities. She knew that years of her bonding with Mili, as it had been till a day ago, could make anyone jealous. Pritha decided that she won't be begging for information. She sat back in her chair and positioned her wrists on the edge of the table.

Vandana looked at Pritha for a few seconds, satisfied that she had extracted enough moments of 'give-me-importance'. Then she began, 'I think Mili is taking wrong decisions. Rohan has told me that she is ready to do anything to continue her relationship with Pankaj.'

'What do you mean "ready to do anything"?'

'Come on! Good girl, at least don't be a dumbhead! Of course, you know what all is involved in a "real" relationship. There is every kind of closeness.'

Pritha was quiet. Her mind was not. *Mili, how can you do this? What are you trying to prove and to whom? You cannot go to such a length with a person you should be getting rid of. And wait a minute! Rohan and... Vandana? I never knew they were friends.*

Rohan was the quintessentially attractive and popular guy in the class. He was not handsome by movie standards, but he was considered smart by consensus among the girls. Every girl wanted to be recognized by him. He was one boy who had as many female friends as male friends. Despite that, he had very limited interaction with Pritha, confined to saying an occasional 'Hi'. Pritha was aware that Rohan had been observing her and that he made no attempt to hide shades of interest in his eyes when he looked at her. There was something in his gaze that made Pritha aware of herself, even though that gaze was most often across a corridor or through reagent shelves in the chemistry lab.

Vandana continued, 'I would have known nothing of this stuff had Rohan not told me. He didn't have your number. So, he asked me to tell you about it. I don't know the details, though. It was so nice of Rohan to have told me this. He is a really nice guy. He wants to save Mili from trouble. How nice, no?'

Ignoring the tedious 'nice', Pritha asked, 'I don't get it, Vandana. How does Rohan know about this...this plan...or whatever?' Pritha struggled to find words for the awkward piece of information.

Pritha had barely finished her sentence when she sensed someone standing near her. She looked up and saw Rohan. *What is he doing here? Is this some kind of a grand conspiracy against me and Mili? Gosh! I am confused.*

'Hi. Can I sit with you, girls?' Rohan asked.

Pritha stayed quiet but Vandana gave an instant, screechy reply, 'Of course!' Pritha noticed a hint of a blush on Vandana's face.

Rohan looked at the two unoccupied chairs. The one next to Vandana had her huge purple bag on it. Just as she stretched out her hand to pick it up, Rohan quickly took the seat next to Pritha. Pritha gathered her arms close to herself. She tried to make sense of the whole scenario. *Why are these people concerned about anything related to Mili? Are they even telling me the truth? What is Mili up to? Gosh, did I apply the deodorant this morning?* Pritha had gotten ready in a flash and she could not remember how well she had done her hair or even if she had looked at herself in the mirror properly. She looked at the drink in front of her. It was full of calories. *What am I thinking of! What do I care about what he thinks!* Perhaps, he wouldn't even observe.

Pritha felt uncomfortable with her thoughts. In Rohan's company, she was paying unusual attention to herself. *I should be worried about Mili right now.* She took out her phone from her bag, though she did not know what she wanted to do with it. She just looked at the screen and wondered what to do.

After a few seconds of silence, Rohan began speaking to Pritha in a soft, comforting tone, 'Pritha, I know, it sounds kind o' weird that we hardly know each other and yet, I am talking to you about your best friend. You see, Pankaj and I are friends. A few days ago, he said plainly to me that he has no real interest in

Mili.' Rohan noticed a hint of dislike on Pritha's face and added hastily, 'You know, actually, he is not a bad guy, but some boys take things casually.'

Pritha looked into Rohan's eyes, trying to judge his intentions. *Was he trying to help? Or, was he pretending to be a saviour like Vandana, grabbing an opportunity to feel superior in other people's moments of disgrace?*

Rohan continued, 'Listen, Pankaj is taking advantage of Mili. It is Mili's desperation to stick to him that is putting ideas into Pankaj's head.' Rohan cleared his throat and added, 'I have information that he has even booked a hotel room at Circle Road for this evening. And…Mili would be joining him.'

Pritha was shocked and at the same time, she felt ashamed in a vague way. Despite the previous day's events, she was closer to Mili than to anyone else on this planet. She looked at Vandana, trying to explore her purpose of getting involved in this. *What is brewing inside her mind? Is she telling the truth?* She looked at Rohan. He gave her the kind of protective look a nursery teacher would give to her anxious ward and continued softly, 'I tried to dissuade Pankaj from taking advantage of a girl, but he reasons that Mili is with him in this.'

Pritha got up without saying anything. Rohan stood up and pulled back his chair to make way for her. As she took her bag, Rohan asked in a grave voice, 'I know it is tough for you, Pritha. Is there any way I can be of help?'

Pritha took a deep breath, looked at Rohan and said, 'Thanks for telling me about this and for being so concerned. But I'll manage from here on.' She turned to leave, but paused and stepped back, close to Rohan. She looked into his eyes and said in a concrete voice, 'Listen, I value the fact that you gave me this information, but don't pity either Mili or me. Anybody can make an error of judgment.'

A stunned Rohan parted his lips, attempting to say something, but words failed him. Pritha next looked at Vandana, 'I must tell you pretty straight that Mili is a great girl. At this moment, she is slightly misguided. Thank you for the information, anyways. I value that.'

Pritha walked out of the canteen, leaving the two staring after her. As she walked along the corridor to the garden, she made quick calculations in her mind. She hadn't seen Mili in the college that day. For sure, Mili hadn't come to college. Pritha held her phone, unsure whether to call up Mili. *Anyhow, it would be useless to call her. She either won't pick up the phone or would not talk to me. I would have to wait until the evening.*

∽

Circle Road was one of the quieter places in the town, even at six in the evening. Unlike the other roads of the town that were invariably flanked by shops, markets or other commercial structures, Circle Road had a few odd shops on the stretch of the road just outside the railway station. It was here that all the four hotels with the address 'Circle Road' were situated. The road got its name from the way it formed a perfect circle around the base of a mountain. It was the mountain on which the temple was situated.

Pritha looked out from the full-length glass window of a small pastry shop on the road. She stood close to the window and could see a substantial part of the road from that place. The town had quite a few such eateries where one could have a quick snack, usually a patty, a pastry or juice. Pritha had paid for the juice carton in her hand and took small sips from it, constantly keeping a watch on the part of the road to her left, which led to Mili's locality. Pritha usually did not come out of her home in late evenings, but she had told her mother that she was going to meet Mili. She hoped it wouldn't turn out to be a lie.

A strong aroma of incense caused Pritha to turn around and

look at where it was coming from. The shop owner had lighted incense sticks in the small temple in the shop, a ritual which most shopkeepers performed once in the morning and once in the evening. The 'temple' was a little cabinet amongst numerous other shelves on the wall. The man folded his hands in prayer to the row of small idols placed in the cabinet. Then he picked up one of the idols, turned it around in his hand and put it on the counter. He called out to his helper, 'Babulal, you will be going home early today. So, take this idol with you and place it at a proper place. How the colour has faded! Do you know where it should be placed?'

The helper, a short man with curly black hair paused his task of stacking biscuit packets and came towards his employer. He replied in a small, servile voice, 'Yes, I know. It should be placed under a peepul tree or in a temple.' At this, he folded his hands and bowed before the idol seated on the counter. Pritha, who had been observing this dialogue, wondered how curly the helper's hair was. The long length of his hair only emphasized the curliness more. She turned and resumed her observation of the road. Occasionally, a vehicle passed along the road, breaking the silence with a roar. There weren't many passers-by on the road either, just about one or two people every few minutes.

Out of curiosity, Pritha glanced back at the idol. It was half-smeared in dull red colour, perhaps due to the vermillion that had been applied on it every day. The helper would take it somewhere. *Where?* She felt like asking the shopkeeper how he would feel after removing one of the 'gods' from his shop, a god he had been worshipping every day. She took another sip of juice and turned her focus back on to the road.

Pritha almost forgot to swallow the mouthful as she saw Mili turn around the corner of the road. *Of course, I knew she would come, but then why am I still shocked to see her?* Mili was carrying a couple of books in her hand. She obviously had to pretend, as in this small town, almost everybody knew everybody, and one never could tell who was watching. Mili stood at the side of the road, around twenty metres away from the shop inside which Pritha was waiting. She was careful not to stand next to any hotel. Pritha threw her juice carton into the trash bin and went closer to the glass door.

She waited with bated breath till she saw Pankaj turn up on his bike. Two of his friends were riding pillion, all three without helmets. The silent road roared once again with the sound of the motorcycle. Pankaj rode past Mili without looking at her and parked his bike a good distance away from where she was standing. Mili looked away, pretending not to notice him. Anyone could be watching, so they had to keep pretending. Pritha had never liked the way Pankaj dressed: ripped jeans and most of the times, sleeveless shirts with horror-theme graphics. She most detested his shoes with pointed toes. Pritha looked at Mili's face. There was a cunning, stupid shyness on her face as she saw the three approaching. *What has happened to you Mili? Don't you realize what you are going to do?* Then Pankaj started walking towards a slip road that led to the hotels. A moment later, Mili started following them, keeping a good distance.

Pritha dashed out of the pastry shop and walked fast towards Mili. The latter turned around and her face went blank when she saw Pritha. She stopped walking and almost shouted, 'Why are you here?' Pankaj and his friends stopped and looked up in confusion. Pritha stood face to face with Mili and spoke.

'I will not waste time in asking you what you are doing here. Don't explain anything and don't assume that I am spying on you. Get back home.' Pritha looked intently into Mili's eyes, wanting to use harsh words. But she quickly softened a little and added, 'Please…'

Pritha waited for a few seconds, looking at Mili apprehensively. When Mili did not respond, she said sternly, 'I want to talk to you. Should I say things in front of them or would you come with me?' By this time, the boys had come closer and were standing behind Mili.

Mili stayed silent. Her breathing became deeper, and she narrowed her eyes to look at Pritha. Pritha knew that Mili had felt a pang of discomfort. A process had started. For all the differences in the world, the two were a mirror to each other. The moment Mili looked at Pritha, she could see the shallowness of her own impulsive behaviour. Pritha continued looking at Mili, waiting for a response, but soon her patience wore out. She clenched her fist behind her and looked at Pankaj who was standing opposite her. Pankaj gave a matter-of-fact glance at Pritha and started rolling his thumb over his phone screen while the other two boys looked on as if enjoying an entertaining spectacle.

Mili too turned her eyes away from Pritha and looked at Pankaj. Her eyes expected something. Pankaj glanced at her but kept rolling his thumb over his phone. No one else but Pritha could understand what that expression in Mili's eyes meant. *Foolish Mili, do you actually think this guy will come and stand by you?*

After a couple of minutes of this awkwardness, Pritha blurted out, 'Ask yourself what you are doing, Mili. You have frozen your brain somewhere and you are moving around hollow-headed.' She held Mili's hand and said, 'Come with me.'

Mili tore off from Pritha, went up to Pankaj and looked in his eyes. Then, without looking at Pritha, she said, 'Pritha, I have come to meet him. You have no job here and you should leave.'

'Meet whom?' Pritha half-shouted.

She went straight up to the two, ignored Mili this time and looked up at Pankaj. 'Is Mili your girlfriend?'

There was a long pause. Everybody looked at Pankaj. Two men passing by slowed down and stared at the group and then walked away. Pritha saw that one of those men was the curly-haired shop assistant who quickly turned away his gaze. Pankaj rolled his eyes and said, 'You have no business asking me questions.'

From the corner of her eye, Pritha could see the shadow of pain that had started to appear on Mili's face.

'You have to answer me because I am her friend and I would be the one announcing your engagement to the public: the class, her friends and her family. I would be so happy to do that.' She noticed the uneasiness on Pankaj's face and decided to enhance it.

'You must tell me. Mili and I spend a lot of time together. I'll then stop intruding into her time so that she can spend more time with you. Wow, won't it be great if the two of you decide to spend the rest of your lives with each other? Oh God! I'll have to make arrangements for your engagement…dress, make-up and all. I would be so happy!' Pritha achieved what she had been wanting; Pankaj's face twisted in dislike. She added emphatically, 'So, I have a right to know if you are committed to each other.'

By now, Pankaj had been running his hand through his hair in frustration. He half-shouted, 'Where does the question of commitment come from? This matter is between me and Mili. You are no one to interfere.'

'Are you committed to her?' Pritha said calmly but loudly.

'Nonsense! Why is she meddling in this?' He turned in irritation towards Mili. By this time, Mili's face had been covered with a steady trickle of tears, falling straight from her eyes, touching the plumpness of her cheeks and falling on the books she tightly clenched in her hands.

Pritha swallowed hard. She could feel Mili's heartache in her chest. She had to continue inflicting this pain on Mili, like a surgeon trying to remove a bullet lodged in a patient's body, without anaesthesia. She continued, 'If you are her boyfriend, you will remain loyal and committed in the relationship. Right?'

'Loyal? Nonsense! I'm not a pet! What kind of muck are we talking about here…?' Pankaj waved his hands violently in the air. Mili covered her mouth with her hand and tried to stifle a sob while Pankaj looked at her in annoyance. Mili gained slight control of herself, looked at Pankaj and spoke in a muffled voice, 'It's over now. What never was…is over now…'

Mili walked away from the group, increasing her speed with every step. Pritha started after Mili, keeping a distance. She was not sure whether she should approach Mili at this time. The three boys were left standing on the road. Pankaj put his hands in his pockets and looked in the direction of the girls. There was a short pause when one of his friends blurted, 'Gosh! She was too smart, man, that Pritha. She was too smart!'

The other added, 'Such girls scare me, buddy. You can't play with them. They carry their brains and their guts together.'

∞

Pritha kept her eyes on Mili as she followed the latter down the road. It was getting dark and even lonelier on the road. Pritha could sense Mili's intense pain but, surprisingly for her, the dominant feeling was that of relief. She had been able to save her friend from landing into a dirty muddle.

Mili would perhaps never talk to me again. Wait a minute… where is she heading?

Pritha saw Mili taking the road up the hill rather than the road towards her home. Alarmed, she shouted, 'Mili…'

Mili heard the call but quickened her pace without looking back. She walked briskly on the road that led to the mountaintop temple. Pritha walked faster, unable to understand where Mili could be going. Then a thought struck her mind. *Gosh! She is hurt and badly upset. What is she trying to do? Why is she going uphill in the darkness? Goodness, no, she cannot kill herself! No, Mili, you cannot kill yourself!*

Every nerve in Pritha's head felt tense. She ran after Mili as fast as she could.

5

Murder?

Pritha started running uphill on the road leading to the temple. She strained her eyes to locate Mili. The darkness of the early night was settling down on everything, minimizing visibility. The path was even darker as there were barely any streetlights. Of course, people were not expected to go up the road to the temple after dark. To add to it, the winding road made it even more difficult for Pritha to see how far Mili had gone.

She ran as fast as the slope allowed her to. *What if she ends her life? Don't do this, Mili! I was only trying to save you from a huge mess. You were blinded and I could not bear to see you in trouble, even though you might not want to have anything to do with me now.* Pritha wished she could shout out her thoughts to Mili, and that she would listen. The road was narrow. On one side, it was flanked by a wall of thick shrubs that grew on the mountain soil. Snakes lurking in such shrubs were common in the hills. At night, these reptiles often ventured out of their hideouts for a slithery stroll on the roads. Humans would ideally walk slowly and with full watchfulness in such areas, stopping instantly in case a snake wanted to cross the road first. Pritha could not afford to slow down. She looked to her left, at the road below. A short iron fence secured the road along this side. A slip through the gaps of the fence would take one several feet down on to Circle Road.

Pritha tried to move fast, looking ahead in desperation for

Mili's figure. She hadn't encountered any person on the road yet, when her eyes suddenly fell on something white and bright along the side of the road. The aster flowers shining in the moonlight reminded Pritha of the temple. She slowed down for an instant, confused as to why Mili was heading that way. The short pause was helpful, as in the silence, she could hear footsteps ahead of her. Pritha was now sure that someone was moving ahead of her. It was getting darker, too late to stay out without informing her family. For sure her mother would call up. Pritha put her phone on silent mode. She didn't want Mili to know she was following her. That might agitate her and she could make a rash decision, perhaps even jump down... Pritha shuddered.

She had advanced uphill for more than fifteen minutes now but did not catch a glimpse of Mili. Her throbbing heart pounded so heavily inside her chest that it slackened her pace. Yet, she moved as silently and as fast as she could. Partly exhausted, she paused for breath and looked up. She was almost at the top of the hill. She could see the pillars to the entrance of the temple compound.

In a flash, she saw someone entering the gate of the temple. Was it Mili? It was hard to say but Pritha calculated that she had seen no one else on this road so far. So, it would be Mili, no one else. *It is several metres down below; it is impossible for someone to survive that fall from the top. If there is a God in that temple, please let her be saved!* Pritha had never felt so desperate in her life. If there was a God, perhaps, he or she would listen to her. In those few seconds of extreme fear, the innumerable moments she had spent with Mili sped past her eyes. There were moments of pure fun and moments of momentous discussions. In her anxiety, countless glimpses of their life together flashed like a movie before her eyes.

Pritha felt a mild pain in her chest. Her heart was throbbing even more violently now. She took a deep breath, taking in cool air. The anxiety was crushing, but it was a young heart, strong and ready for challenges. She reminded herself to be calm and decided to move quietly, trying not to make any sounds. Her sneakers would be just right for this. She feared Mili would hasten her steps if she saw Pritha around. Even if Mili was standing at the edge of the mountain, Pritha thought she would quietly move behind her and hold her with all her strength. She would do anything in the universe to stop her friend from ending her life. Pritha trembled at the realization about the kind of words floating in her mind.

She entered through the open gateway of the temple compound, careful not to walk under the lights. She kept to the darker sides of the pathway. The compound appeared to be deserted.

Pritha's eyes scanned the area for Mili. *This is the mountaintop. Where is she?* She reached the side of the main hall of the temple and entered the garden area. Light came out from the huge windows of the temple hall and lit parts of the garden area. The outer walls of the hall were dark with the building's shadow. There was some commotion inside but Pritha ignored it. She stayed in the darker areas with her back to the wall. She felt the vibration of the phone in her trouser pocket. It would be her mother calling. *Gosh! It is too late. I should have been at home by this time.* She softly took out the phone and texted her mother, telling her she would be back in some time. Pritha got a strange pang of discomfort in the chest at the thought of things not going quite right. Quickly, she shrugged off the thoughts and looked around again, moving softly. *Did Mili even come here? How could I damn forget that there are at least two slip roads away from the road to the top of the mountain? But I saw her entering the compound... Or was it Mili at all...?*

A frantic shriek from inside the temple hall startled Pritha out of her thoughts. She jumped in fear but soon realized that it was not a female voice. Sweat trickled down her shirt. She sprung up to the window and peeked inside. Two temple priests were holding a man by his arms just as the latter hunkered down on the floor, crying and scared. Pritha slid to a side, moving herself out of sight. She peeped in again, trying to keep only her eyes in the range of the window. She could see the rage on the faces of the priests. She looked more carefully at the crouching man. He had curly hair. He was pleading with folded hands and was gesturing at something on the floor. From that distance of at least seven metres, she could see that there was a small object on the floor... It was the idol smeared with red colour. *He is the assistant at the pastry shop! He must have come here to place the idol.*

'Please let me go, please! I am a poor man. I live in the worker's slums, sir, and toil day and night to feed my family...' The man pleaded desperately.

One second, Pritha wanted to move away, but the other, she wanted to see what was going on. After a few seconds of confusion, she stayed and looked on. A third priest entered the hall. The cries of the man on the floor got louder. While one priest held the man down, the other one picked up a long piece of red cloth from the altar and wrapped it tightly around the man's mouth. The cries got subdued. The man tried desperately to free himself. Pritha felt an urge to run into the hall and save the man, but fear had glued her feet to the ground. She saw the third priest handing over something to one of the two men. It was too small to be a gun...it was not a gun that was handed over. It was a syringe. Pritha froze.

The priest loaded the syringe from a vial, shouted something at the man and injected the fluid into his neck. The man wriggled like a worm for a few seconds and then fell on the floor. Pritha moved away from the window. She could feel nothing except her heart pounding destructively on her rib cage. Sweat soaked her shirt. Her hands shook violently. Her parched throat didn't allow her to swallow her own saliva. She stood there for a couple of minutes that seemed like hours to her, unable to comprehend anything.

Slowly, she tried to move her feet. Her head was burning with stress. Mechanically, she glanced once more through the window. The man with curly hair lay like a sack on the floor. The three priests were engaged in a conversation. Pritha's senses reminded her of the need to get out of this place. Without thinking, she set back on the same path that she had taken to come into the temple complex. She moved slowly, unaware whether her steps were making any noise or not. She felt numbness in her body as well as her thinking. *Was it so easy to take the life out of a man? I am breathing now but in another few seconds, I could be lying on the floor like a sack... What if somebody had seen me there?* She wanted to believe no one had noticed her presence. As she stepped out of the gate, she looked back, her breath caught inside her lungs. Her heart was ready to crack her ribs. She scanned the area with her eyes. No one was there. No one dared enter that place after dark. She walked downhill towards Circle Road.

No one entered the temple after dark, except the priests who had special initiation to do so. This is what the town was told, and everybody followed it. There were stories of a few people who had done so and had met with death in the temple. No one messed with divinity. *I was there too. I had peeped into the temple... Where is Mili?*

Her mind numbed in shock, Pritha proceeded down the road. A few metres along, an uneasy sensation started to grow inside her. It was a creepy feeling that there was something behind her; somebody was following her. It was as if she was being tracked by someone who did not want her to get away. Her breath became heavy. Her steps became heavy. She thought she was moving through sand. She thought any moment, something or someone that was moving towards her would suddenly pounce upon her and would smother her. The feeling grew with each step. She dare not turn around. She tried to run but her feet moved slowly. She almost tripped over a large stone that lay in the path. She balanced herself and, in that instant, rediscovered her own capacity to run away from danger, her capacity to have control over her movement. She started running.

In the next couple of minutes, she reached a brighter part of the road where a yellow streetlight threw its dim light around. The speed of her movement gave her a fraction of courage to turn her head around and see what was following her. Her heart took a bigger leap when she turned her head around. At that moment, she could not comprehend what she saw. She blinked her eyes and looked more keenly. No one was visible on the road. The moonward side of the hill glistened in the moonlight. There was no one around.

She decided to keep running until she reached the bottom of the hill. Her head was heavy as it had never been. *Who are those priests? What did they…?* Pritha almost choked. The vision of the sack-of-a-man on the floor stuck to her mind. *Why did he have to go there at this time? For sure he was the curly-haired attendant from the pastry shop.*

The sudden vibration of her mobile phone startled her. She received her mother's call with shaking hands and told her mechanically she would be back in half an hour and disconnected the call.

6

The Monster

Pritha had never felt as numb in her life as she did during that thirty-minute walk to her home. At the lonelier stretches of the route, there was an overpowering feeling of being followed; a strange feeling that someone or something was following her, and it was moving at a steady pace. As she opened the gate to the lawn in front of her house, she expected the feeling to go away. Strangely, it did not. She rang the doorbell hastily and when her father opened the door, she found her house overflowing with sounds of a party-like atmosphere. Her maternal uncle and aunt had unexpectedly dropped in and Pritha's parents were too delighted and were busy with the guests. Pritha looked at the sky and felt thankful for this perfect diversion that would save her the discomfort of facing her parents in this mental state. She greeted the guests, exchanged the necessary pleasantries and excused herself for some time.

Pritha shut the door of her room behind her and quickly called up Mili's landline number. Enough time had passed for Mili to get back home and if she had not, it was high time her parents knew about it. Mili's father answered the phone. He said Mili was not well and was asleep in her room. Pritha wanted to hear that once again, to be doubly sure that Mili was safe, so she asked if Mili had a fever or something. Her father said that she seemed to be simply tired. Pritha sunk down on the floor beside her bed, breathing deeply. She said a faint 'thank you' and disconnected the call. She felt the heaviness of tears in her eyes, the drops brimming, ready to trickle down, but she held them back.

She is safe. She is safe. She is safe! Pritha whispered to herself. She felt an uncontrolled urge to envelope Mili in a bear hug. The latter would perhaps not do the same ever again. Yet Pritha looked up and wanted to thank somebody…would it be God, the stars, fate or whatever… She knew none nor had experienced any of them personally. She decided to sit in silence for some moments, to sink into the feeling of relief. How she had feared for Mili's life!

The sounds of the family chatter in the living room reminded her of the need to join them without much delay.

Pritha got up and looked around the room. It was silent, but a faint hissing sound seemed to be circulating in the air outside. That uneasiness of being watched returned. She looked at the window. It was shut and none of the glass panes was broken. Pritha had a feeling something was trying to get in, to get closer to her. It was as if a huge jelly monster had been slithering down the road behind her and now, it had expanded and enveloped her house, looking for a suitable hole through which it could get in. She felt uneasy about her own thoughts. *Perhaps, I am too tired.*

She freshened up, changed into her night suit and went into the living room. The relief about Mili's safety had given her a tiny bit of normalcy that would enable her to behave with reasonable routine with the family. Her parents would be too busy with the guests to notice anything strange about her. Pritha had never imagined how difficult it was to live in two worlds, one in the mind and the other out there. When she tried to eat or drink, the scene at the temple started floating before her eyes. The vision had apparently fixed itself to her mind permanently.

It was eleven in the night when Pritha entered her room after dinner. Perhaps she should have told her parents, but her mother would go insane at the thought of her daughter going to the temple at the forbidden time. Moreover, what would she think of Mili? Beena would brand Mili as a 'girl of questionable character' or something similar.

A pang of loneliness dug at Pritha's heart. She sat down on her study chair, looking at the window. She could go out and talk to the moon, as she had done numerous times, but she did not have the strength to leave her house that night. There was something lingering around, something that was making her uneasy. She just wanted to curl up in her bed. She sat down on the bed with her back against the headboard, pulled up the sheets and covered her legs, waited a moment and then pulled the sheet up to her shoulders. She folded her knees close to her chest and wrapped her arms around them.

What is going on? What could I do? That helpless man! I can't speak to my parents. I can't speak to my friend. Can I keep it all to myself? Should I keep it to myself? Pritha looked through all the objects in her room, not seeing anything, only thinking. *Who were those people? Are they really some kind of messengers of divine justice? What is it about no one being allowed into the shrine at night? What about me? Did I do something forbidden? What about that poor man?* Pritha started getting even more uneasy. She glanced at the window. *What is this strange thing around my house?*

Pritha felt her head getting heavier. The only moments of stress she had faced in her life before this night were either her disagreements with her parents, or not having finished her course before an exam. For a teenager living a typical life, the events of that day were too heavy to bear. Pritha stretched out her hand to switch off the lights, lingered for a few seconds and then brought her hand back into the sheet without switching off the lights. She slid down on her pillow and did not remember when sleep overtook her tired mind.

She woke up in the morning to the sound of rapid knocking at the closed window. The sound of a whistle from the pressure cooker in the kitchen made her glance at the clock. Her parents must have been up for some time now. She clutched her pillow and put her feet down on the floor. In a flash, she withdrew her feet, curled up once again on the bed, bent down and looked closely at the floor, her heart pounding with anxiety. There was nothing suspicious there. She stood up reluctantly, still clutching the pillow close to her chest. The fervent knocking was repeated on the windowpane. Pritha stared at the curtain that hid the windowpane, still standing close to her bed. The shadow of a non-human shape formed by the sunlight was visible on the curtain. Pritha sighed in relief. It was the usual mynah that mistook its own reflection in the glass for another bird.

She drew aside the curtain and looked at the sunlit trees through the closed window. Her gaze returned to her room and thoughts of the previous evening flooded back into her mind. In a moment, the scene outside her window seemed to be enveloped in a strange kind of slime; a slimy monster covered everything around her. Pritha forced herself to get up from the bed and to free herself of this weird feeling. *How can my thinking get so illogical? How can there be a 'monster' waiting for me outside? No, but the feeling is real...it is real.* No one could be following her since last night and even if someone really was, he could not melt himself into an entity that surrounded her entire house.

A few minutes later, Pritha entered the living room. Her parents, aunt and uncle sat on the sofas, looking tense. Her father had a cup of tea in his hand while the other cups lay unfinished on the coffee table. Beena was reading the newspaper intently. Pritha's aunt, sitting next to Beena, also peered with curiosity at the newspaper. There was a gloomy silence in the room.

'Good morning...' Pritha said hesitatingly.

The four looked up and mumbled a quick 'morning'.

'Is everything okay?'

Pritha's mother gestured towards the newspaper. 'How can everything be okay, child, when people don't have any regard for religious rules? Where is the world heading to? Temples are places to be respected. If you break the rules, God is definitely going to be angry.'

Pritha looked questioningly at her mother.

Beena took a deep breath, passed on the open newspaper to her sister. She folded her hands and looked at the ceiling, muttered something and said, 'A man committed the sin of entering the holy mountaintop temple after dark, and in the morning, he was found paralyzed on the temple floor.'

'Paralyzed?' Pritha almost shouted.

'Yes, he is breathing, but he cannot speak and cannot move his hands and legs. That is the price one pays for interfering with divine rules.'

Her uncle added, 'Once a similar thing had happened in...' Pritha did not hear what he went on to describe. She felt her mind journeying into a deep cave of confusion, like into a whirlpool. She could see herself enveloped in a grey muddle she could not free herself from. A vortex of unanswered questions gorged upon her. The monster seemed to be closing in upon her. She was going deeper into the whirlpool...

'Amu, dear, once you get ready, come and help me in the kitchen please.' Beena's voice pulled back Pritha to the real world. Pritha nodded. She took the newspaper from the table and hurriedly read the news report. It carried a statement from the leader of the temple committee: 'A grave sin has been committed by the man who entered the temple. God has punished him for his sin. We, human beings, should not interfere in the rules set by the Divine. Since it was an auspicious day of the full moon yesterday,

God has spared the sinner's life. Otherwise, we know of worst instances. We will perform special rituals in the temple to rid it of the impurities that have polluted it because of that man's sin. The deity is furious, and all the people of the town must perform rituals to avoid ill-fate. Priests will be available to guide everyone on how to perform the rituals.'

The last part of the statement held great importance for Beena. For years, she had accorded the temple a position of supreme authority in her life. She too believed in the rumours that ill fate would befall anyone who ventured into the temple after dark. The news report had lent a fresh reason for the town to believe in this stuff, for the people had absolute faith in whatever statements came from the temple.

Beena's voice held a sense of urgency as she spoke to the people around her, 'We will have to do the corrective things today itself. One of my friends will get all the information about the fasts, the offerings and whatever needs to be done.'

Pritha's aunt added, 'One man commits a sin and the whole town pays for it. Di, you should prioritize purifying your home.'

Pritha's mother nodded in complete agreement. She went to the dining table, pulled out a chair and sat down. She started typing out messages to her friends. Pritha knew the temple would be thronged by people who would be visiting the priests.

There would be crowds, in swarms, in the temple premises. The sounds of the imagined crowds rose in swirls in Pritha's mind, increasing in intensity as they went higher. There were the scared voices of women, the concerned voices of men and the didactic voices of the priests. No one in the universe except Pritha heard a voice that came from the pit of the swirls. It was the stifled cry of a man, helpless, pleading desperately. Sweat trickled down Pritha's temples and fell on her hand. Her thoughts dashed to the present, to the living room of her house.

She looked closely at her mother, then at her father and at the guests. *False beliefs! False notions! I wouldn't have cared what they think of all this had I not seen the truth myself. I was sure that man would die. I thought they had injected poison. He survived!* Pritha walked up to the dining table and sat on a chair next to her mother. She watched a fully engrossed Beena sharing text messages on the phone. *I must tell her that the man was attacked and that...I saw it.* At this thought, Pritha's heart started beating violently and hurt the inside of her chest. Sweat rolled freely down her neck. She got up and headed to her room.

7

Fear

Pritha rushed to her room and hastily closed the door behind her. She paced around the small room, breathing heavily. She felt desperate to shout out the truth, to tell the world what she had seen; what only she had seen. She wanted to scream, she wanted to tell her family the truth. If only she could smoothly broadcast her thoughts to the entire town. *I must, I must tell the people they are being misled.* The thought pricked Pritha's mind from every direction. Yet, she could not bring herself to reveal the truth to her mother or her father, not yet. They wouldn't believe her.

An animated collage of images swam incessantly before her eyes: images of the temple, the newspaper and the previous night. The muffled sounds of the victim buzzed like a swarm of honeybees in her head. Pritha slumped down on the floor, rested her back against the bed and closed her eyes. She visualized herself approaching her mother and telling her about what she had seen at the temple.

Telling Ma would be fruitless! She won't believe me. Faith in the temple was rooted in Beena's psyche. She would dismiss the news as a teenager's prank. But that would come later. The mere mention of Pritha having gone up the temple in the dark would plunge Beena into depression. Fear, anxiety and guilt would engulf her, numbing her sense of reasoning. That her daughter had committed the gravest sin would be too much of a shock for Beena.

No, facts are not for Ma, not yet. Wait a minute, what if she believes I saw the attack at the temple? Pritha thought long about it. That scenario might be even more troublesome. For her mother, the primary concern would be that her daughter was involved in a supposed sin. Period. To counter that, Pritha might be confined to home, and worse, she would be subjected to a series of 'purification' rituals. Equally bad would be the assumptions Beena would form about Mili. For sure, she would brand Mili with some kind of a clichéd title like 'a loose character' or a 'bad girl' or something. Pritha would have to leave aside Mili's story. She would have to cook up another reason for going uphill. What would it be? Whatever reason she would give, her mother would be a candidate for depression that would perhaps last all her life.

Yet, there is a chance Mom would take it as it is. That would rid her of her obsession with the temple and its priests and the superstitions associated with them. Pritha thought deeply, trying to figure out that possibility. Even if Beena's blind faith in the temple was cured, she knew her mother and her father were people who would not confront the society, normally. They were mild people, who believed in ignoring a lot of things. They would be the last people on earth to fight against the belief of an entire town. In that case, they would force Pritha to keep quiet on the issue. Who knows, they might even want to leave that town forever. The truth would never be known in that case.

Pritha thought of the easiest thing to do: stay silent, forget everything and get back to normal. What if she did not tell anybody anything about it? Things would go on as usual. She would go to college, come back and do the routine stuff. As Pritha visualized this possibility on the screen of her mind, her being was flooded with a bitter sea of dissatisfaction, a sea of never-ending waters with an obnoxious smell and an acrimonious taste. *How will I live with that feeling, that cancerous feeling? I saw it...I saw the attack. There was no divine role in that. Those cruel priests only wanted to prove a point. They only wanted to project a myth as truth. And… they have succeeded. Gosh, they have succeeded! I know, perhaps only I know what the facts are. I won't let them get away with this.*

Just as this thought flitted past Pritha's mind, she looked through the window. The feeling of being watched, of being followed, had started subsiding. The monster was gradually losing its power. It could no longer envelope the house; it could no longer barge into the house. It was as if the monster had lost its vigour and was now reduced to a dwarf that could cling to the window but could not attack.

Pritha still looked through the window, wondering at how her dehydrated senses had started regaining a bit of their energy. She stared at the floor, deep in thought, when a shiny blue beetle on the floor caught her eye. It crawled around, probably trying to find its destination. Pritha placed her palm in the insect's path. It climbed up without hesitation, as if it didn't differentiate what material its path was made of as long as it took it somewhere. Pritha closed in her fingers to encase the beetle in a momentary prison. She stood up and went to the window, pushed down the latch and opened it. She then extended her hand to open it as wide as possible. Slowly, she opened up her fist to release the beetle into the garden outside. However, the insect shot out its wings and made a brave flight back into the room. It headed straight to the cupboard and landed on a yellow sticky note. Pritha went to the cupboard and saw the tiny creature sitting happily on the piece of paper. *Strange! It doesn't want to set itself free!*

Pritha looked at her cupboard. She had a habit of copying quotations from famous people, or extracts from literature that she liked. She wrote these on sticky notes and pasted them on her cupboard. This one activity she loved, despite what others thought of it. She had been greatly irritated when one of her cousins, Amrit, had called this habit 'old-fashioned kids' stuff' and had jokingly named the collection 'Alibaba's scrapbook'. Pritha did consider it as a treasure-board where she thought she had pasted the best words ever written. She didn't care a damn about what others thought of it as long as she felt happy about it.

She recalled her cousins Amrit and Simran, who used to come visiting during every summer vacation till they reached higher classes. It used to be fun. Pritha recalled how the three of them played around all day and when the visitors left after a few days, she was struck with that stabbing feeling of not having a sibling. Consequently, she would persuade her mother to let her spend long hours at Mili's house.

It was one such summer day when her cousins, aunt and uncle were staying with them that an incident had occurred. The family was in the living room when they were startled with loud shrieks from the verandah. It was Simran, then just a five-year-old. Everyone had rushed out to see her huddled against the wall, crying and perspiring. When she saw her mother, she had clung to her and shivered with fear. However, she had not told the reason why she was so frightened.

On repeated efforts, Simran had pointed out a finger in the direction of the walkway and had murmured, 'Demon…Monster…' Then she had started crying even more loudly. Everyone had looked around, alarmed. What they saw was just a bunch of long human hair, entangled in dry grass blades, moving in a circular, vigorous motion because a good breeze was blowing. The air struck the walls of the verandah and deflected to cause the bunch to circle in that corner against the wall. Everyone had heaved a sigh of relief and had even laughed at the child's imagination. Pritha, around ten years of age at that time, understood what Simran was going through. The elders had simply told the child that it was nothing. But Pritha had gone up and had stopped the movement of the bunch, using a stick. She had then spread out the hair and the grass and had asked Simran to see it for what it actually was. The child had stopped sobbing after that.

Pritha thought of the present time and recognized the suffocation her whole being was feeling. She looked at the small pink, blue and yellow sticky notes. How easy it was to copy somebody else's observations! *How easy it was to feel like a champion when there was no challenge.*

Pritha felt a twinge of shame inside her. She had always thought of herself as a person who wouldn't think twice before doing the right thing, even if it was confronting the most powerful people in the world. She recalled the history lessons in school that had often fired in her a desire to fight against injustice. While reading about revolutions and about freedom movements, she had often daydreamt of going back in time, of being the heroine in the fight against injustice and oppression.

How easy it was to imagine oneself as a heroic figure who was born to set things right! Now, standing powerless before the witnesses of her heroic aspirations, for the first time, she wished somebody would shout out to her 'Ahoy, Queen of Jhansi'. She realized how childish her daydreams of bravery had been. Right now, she felt smothered; she felt helpless. That disgusted her. For the nineteen years of her life, the last thing she had wanted was to feel weak and helpless. She looked at the cupboard door. The tiny bits of paper and the words written on them seemed to be mocking her. *Copying inspirational words won't make you courageous, girl! Action would!*

Pritha stood there, deep in thought while the beetle had a leisurely walk from one note to another. *No, I can't spend my life hiding in my room. I can't spend my life with the window closed! I can keep quiet; I can stay away from trouble; I can get old with this secret in my chest; but how will I hide from myself, from my thoughts? They will grow in me like a slow poison. No, for sure, I can't live on like this!*

A light breeze squeezed itself into the room from the open window. Pritha breathed the air consciously and looked at the sunlit garden outside. The monster was melting. It was getting absorbed into the ground. The clouds of suffocation were blowing away. The unseen apparition that had followed her from the temple was evaporating. It was getting dispersed into the air. Its existence was being wiped out.

Pritha felt a burst of energy inside her. The beetle flitted off and on to the window sill. It crept a while on the frame, and then flew away. Pritha whispered after it, 'Thank you!' She ran her hands softly over the sticky notes, thanking these too. As she neared the lower end, her finger stuck to a dog-eared corner of the only green bit of paper. She bent forward and read what she had scribbled on it, months ago. It was a quote from Stephen King:

'Monsters are real, and ghosts are real too. They live inside us, and sometimes, they win.'

8

Disgust

It was ten in the morning when Pritha found herself standing in front of the police station. The sight of the yellow and blue signboard arching above the gate made her gut twitch with nervousness. Of all the places in this town, this was the unlikeliest she would ever have visited, at least until a day ago. She had passed by this gate numerous times but had only noticed the voluminous bougainvillaea vine that overflowed the boundary wall, dangling its branches towards the road. To Pritha, it always seemed as if the dense, chaotic bush was trying to climb over the wall to escape whatever was inside.

Pritha walked into the small courtyard and halted. There was nobody in attendance. She went up a couple of steps into the verandah. The long verandah had a wooden bench flanked by two flowerpots on each side. The geranium plants in these pots grew out of pale soil; clearly, the soil had never touched any manure. An old wooden door left open led into the building from the verandah. The faded yellow paint of the walls, the coloured marble-chip floor and the wooden bench reminded Pritha of her grandfather's accounts of his younger days. There was such an old-world feel about the place that even the birch tree in the courtyard seemed ancient. A man in police uniform emerged from the door and looked at Pritha.

'Yes?'

'I need to file a complaint.'

The man casually gestured towards the room from which he had emerged and walked out of the main gate. Pritha climbed up the steps to the verandah and entered the room. There were two desks with papers and files on each, but no one was around. She sat on a plastic chair by the door. An officer in khaki emerged from an inner room, talking animatedly on his phone. He came and sat behind one of the desks. Pritha stood up and waited for him to finish his call. A few minutes passed but the officer was still on the phone. Pritha sat down on the chair again and glanced at the time on her phone. She had planned to bunk the first two classes and had expected to reach college at least by eleven o'clock.

Pritha recollected the events of the previous evening in her mind, rehearsing how she would tell every minor detail to the police. The officer was still talking on the phone and ignored Pritha's presence. He glanced towards the door and waved his hand at another officer in the doorway, a man with a huge belly that was protruding far beyond what she thought was possible. The latter entered and sat at the second desk. The officer ended his call and began talking to his colleague.

Pritha was confused. Why weren't they paying attention to a visitor? Was she not supposed to be here? Was it the wrong time? Perhaps, schools should introduce students to the functioning of public offices such as a police station. Did she make the right decision in coming here? The two officers were thoroughly enjoying their conversation, ignoring Pritha's presence for their convenience. Pritha fiddled with her cell phone. The contents of the newspaper flooded into her mind again and she stood up with a firm resolve. If she had a complaint, it was the officers' duty to give due attention to it.

'Excuse me, sir.'

The two gave her an uninterested glance.

'I have to lodge a report.'

The policeman who had come earlier reclined back in his chair and gave the girl a casual look. He gestured with his hand towards a chair that lay in front of his desk. Pritha quickly approached the chair and sat down. He opened a large register and took a pen in his hand. Pritha waited patiently, again.

'Hmm...you want to lodge a complaint?'

Pritha nodded. 'Yes sir, I have some information which I think I should report. I hope the police can take some action. It is something I cannot share with my parents because...'

The officer interrupted Pritha's sentence and began 'What is it? Is it rape, molestation or eve-teasing? Go on, tell your story. We are used to girls strolling into the police station with these complaints.' He signalled with his hand towards Pritha's attire: slim jeans and a sleeveless t-shirt. 'Girls don't even wear proper clothes and they simply walk in here complaining about boys. How many complaints have we got in the last week, Sharma?'

Sharma gave a scornful smile and gawked at Pritha. Pritha noticed that her breathing was getting heavier. She looked at the man, shocked. He leaned forward and pretended to mean well. 'Look, we, the police have to work on serious matters like terror attacks, theft, murder, security of VIPs...really serious things, you know. When girls like you don't pay attention to where and when you are going and what you are wearing, trouble will follow you. We can't go after every boy in this town; they are young, and they watch movies and are on the Internet.' He paused, expecting a nod from Pritha but got no response. He then changed the tone of his monologue.

'Do you go to a college or a school? Private tuitions? You seem to be from a good family. Even decent parents these days don't teach their girls what to wear and whom to talk to. What does your father do? You have come alone, no friend with you?'

The ridicule in the officer's voice caused an overwhelming burning sensation inside Pritha's head. She could not find any words to say to the man. She felt sick inside, sick to the core. She looked at the officer. The latter waited for her reply with a look on his face that said, 'Go on, put your piece of dirty story on the pile of dirt we have here, and get out. We'll do nothing about it. We don't want to do anything about it.'

She managed to mumble, 'No, you are misunderstanding. It is something different.' This time, she did not address the man as 'sir'.

'Aha, so it is not about unknown boys. That means you have a complaint about your boyfriend.'

Pritha could not take in any more. The sickness inside had begun to make her feel nauseated. She got up with a jerk and noticed that her hands were shaking with anger. Yet, she gathered her thoughts and looked the officer in the eye and said, 'I had no idea this police station was for a specific category of complaints. Thanks for not listening to what I wanted to tell you.' She turned to leave, went till the doorway and came back a couple of steps. 'Well, even if I had told you about what I had in mind, I am sure, you could have done nothing about it! You simply could not!'

The officer blurted out something in a rude tone, which she paid no attention to and strode out from that ancient building. Out in the courtyard, she noticed a young girl helping a middle-aged woman into the police station. The latter was not in a very healthy condition. Pritha stood aside to give way, though she wanted to warn all females never to enter this place. However, the sickness inside her was ready to burst out like a volcano. She walked out of the gate, feeling as if she had just walked out of the nineteenth century. She ran to the other edge of the road, the feeling of nausea overpowering her. *Today I know what the word 'disgust' actually means.* She felt like she would throw up right there on the road.

To control her urge, she looked up at the huge oak tree beneath which she was standing. The leaves of the oak swayed in the breeze. All the branches of the tree moved in different directions, yet there was a soothing harmony about the tree. Pritha stood still, looking up. Sunlight made some of the leaves shine while others shied away from the brightness and hid in the darker areas. Minutes passed in silence and a gentle wave of freshness began to calm her down.

Slowly, her mind came out of the shock and she started to think with reason. The revulsion for those men started taking the shape of anger. Pritha started walking in the direction of her college. She glanced back at the oak tree and thanked it silently. There was a multitude of thoughts running around in her head. The apparition of the victim at the temple, with utter helplessness on his face, came back rushing to her, as if screaming, begging somebody to do something. Pritha could not recall any other time in her life when she had experienced emotions that were beyond her comprehension. The events of the temple weighed too heavy on her mind and the weight made her head pain on the sides. She saw a vacant rain-shelter on the side of the road and decided to sit there for some time.

Almost every hill town had this structure, a shelter where a couple of benches were fixed on a platform and covered with a brightly coloured tin roof, mounted on pillars. At this time in the morning, hardly anyone sat there. This was in contrast to the evenings when the rain-shelter served as a gossip station for people. The structure stood on the edge of a mountain road, overlooking a valley with rich, dense vegetation. Pritha sat on the bench facing the valley. This had been one of her favourite spots for treating her eyes to the grand spectacle of nature. Other than today, whenever she had looked in that direction, she had wondered how myriad shades of green united to give the impression of one colour from a distance. She looked ahead dryly and opened her sweaty palms. Her thoughts goaded her to stand up and fight, but had no idea in which direction to shout or whom to fight. She pressed her temples with her fingers to ease the pain. She looked down at the valley again. It sloped deep down, but at a distance, it rose up gradually again and became a majestic mountain. Pritha sensed her mind buzzing with gigantic chaos. *I must not let the policemen get away with their behaviour!*

She grabbed her phone and made a quick search for 'women's rights organizations'. She frantically scrolled through the Internet on her phone to find one located in her town, something she did not have great hopes for. The search yielded no results. Pritha made another search, this time with her town's name and found a news item from a vernacular newspaper mentioning an outfit named 'Naari Shakti', that translated into 'women power'. Pritha got up with resolve and headed to the Naari Shakti office. It would be just a ten-minute walk from where she was. Her mind started rehearsing the report she wanted to make. Her steps slowed down. What would she tell them? *No, it is not necessary to tell them why I went to the police station. I would simply say that I went there and they behaved badly. Would that work? Whatever, the policemen should not get away with such behaviour.*

9

Woman

The pain in Pritha's temples started subsiding, as she saw the name 'Naari Shakti – Empowering Women', painted in white on a red signboard. The office was located on the ground floor of a commercial building. High-rise buildings were prohibited in this town, so this one, with five floors, was high enough. Pritha wondered how the organization got sufficient funds to maintain this commercial space.

A crowd of around a hundred women had gathered on the road in front of the building. Their presence had halted the traffic. The cars had to stop, but two-wheeler riders tried to wriggle out through the maze made entirely of women. They navigated ahead, dead slow, one foot on the road, balancing the vehicle as the handle twisted to the right and the left. The sea of women was abuzz with sounds of conversation. Some were holding banners with messages printed on them. Out of curiosity, Pritha walked along the edge of the crowd, trying to read the printed slogans. She saw the first one: 'Women are the World'. She moved ahead and saw another: 'Men Cannot Exist without Women'. Yet another shouted: 'Down with Men'.

Pritha could not help but think how this crowd seemed to be a species of warriors fighting against some weird, cruel aliens. For sure, they were fighting against the creatures called men. Did they want a world without men? She glanced at the building that housed the organization. There weren't any chances that anyone would be inside the office. Everyone must be out here. She decided to wait for some time. She saw a relatively quieter person standing next to her, a girl in her early twenties. Pritha said a polite 'hello'. The girl nodded. Pritha asked her what the gathering was about.

The girl turned full-faced towards Pritha, pride written clearly on her countenance, 'Naari Shakti is taking out a march today.'

'Against what?'

'Against?' the girl did not understand the question.

Pritha clarified, 'I mean, what is the issue?'

'Nothing.'

Pritha exclaimed, 'Nothing?'

The girl gave a stern look to Pritha and said, 'Aren't bad things happening to women all around? This march is a showcase of the power of women.'

Pritha's mind set itself to think. A hundred-something crowd of women marching down the streets...stopping traffic at some places, perhaps hampering the work of the roadside vendors for some time, shouting slogans on the streets and demanding people's attention. For what? What is their goal? Perhaps they would be able to warn men not to misbehave with women. *But how are they going to do this by taking out a shouting march across the town? They are an organization. They must have some reasons and some methods.*

Pritha turned to the girl again and was about to ask another question when she noticed heightened excitement on the girl's face. She looked in the direction in which the girl was looking. A woman, around forty years of age, wearing a brown cotton sari, stood on the steps to the building, which she intended to use as a podium to address the gathering. The woman called the attention of the crowd. The buzzing sounds of chit-chat subsided and all looked at her.

The leader began her speech in a hoarse voice that comes from speaking too much too loudly. She shouted, 'Down with men! Down with men! This is the age of women!' The crowd repeated after her. She raised her hands to quieten the women and began, 'Time has proven again and again that women are supreme. Be it mythology, be it history, be it science, be it geogr...umm.... time has proved over and over again how superior women are.' Pritha let a huge smile escape her lips. *What if she had uttered the word 'geography'? She must be a teacher.*

The leader continued, 'Once again, we have the evidence how men lead to disaster. You all know what happened at the mountaintop temple. A woman would never be the cause of a town's suffering. A woman is the giver of life. It was again a man who committed a sin and plunged this town into danger. A woman is a nourisher, she is a mother, she is compassionate, she is the giver—she can never be the cause of misery. A woman would never do anything to disrespect the temple and its traditions. It was a man who committed that sin.'

Pritha found herself rooted to the ground. *What? Did I actually hear that? What is the relevance of being a woman here?* Pritha looked around. *These women...did they believe what the leader was saying?* She looked at the leader again and noticed that she had paused. A media van had arrived and newspersons were offloading cameras and tripods. At this sight, the crowd started shouting slogans even more vigorously. The lady on the dais adjusted her sari and her hair and waited for the media people to come up to her with their microphone and camera. Pritha inched her way closer to the leader until she was about three metres away from her and watched her face keenly. She saw a glow of delight on the woman's face as the news people progressed in her direction. Pritha noticed how the woman failed to hide a smile that clearly said 'triumph'. Pritha looked around to see if anyone else noticed what she had. The news people adjusted their cameras, wires and microphones while the woman enjoyed the anticipation of the limelight. But the smile on her face shrunk by an inch as the news reporter turned to the crowd instead of coming to her.

The reporter began to give a commentary on the 'massive crowd', the 'charged atmosphere' and the 'changing times', just as the women in the crowd waved at the camera as if posing for photos while on a family holiday. The reporter asked questions randomly to the women in the crowd. The women shouted back vague answers. After a while, the reporter turned towards the leader. The latter readjusted her hair and got ready for the interaction. Pritha looked on with interest, hoping she would get to know the motive of this rally now. The reporter's first question was 'How do you feel about having such a large support group with you?'

The leader had expected a similar question. She shouted out into the mike, 'Well, it is a wonderful feeling to have such a large number of people who think women are better.' She embarked upon an explanation that was sufficiently detailed and repetitive. The reporter cut her speech short with another question, 'What do you think is the age group of the women who have gathered here?'

The leader pursed her lips on being interrupted mid-sentence; she was perhaps in the habit of delivering long speeches. Yet, she gathered her words and answered, 'Yes, yes, women of all ages relate to us. In fact, right from when a girl is born, she is the embodiment of *naari shakti*.' The comment drew loud applause from the crowd and the leader smiled and waved. The reporter asked a couple more questions.

Pritha turned to a woman standing next to her.

'Would there be anyone in the Naari Shakti office right now?'

The woman gave her a look of amazement, as if she wanted to say, 'Why on earth would anyone be present inside the office when the whole action is taking place outside?' She turned her face away without saying anything. Pritha felt a pang of discomfort at being slighted in such a manner, that too by a woman who was participating in a rally without an agenda. Pritha broke away from the crowd, and looked at it from a distance as she walked away. She had a strong urge to teach the policemen a lesson; but what would these women do? They might perhaps charge into the police station, beat up the police officers and shout slogans about the supremacy of women.

I don't want that. I want those men to become empathetic; I want them to understand that people need the help of the police. I don't want a war between men and women. Why should things be gender-categorized at all? She thought deeply and then blurted out, 'Gosh!' Her mind raced through the events of the past one hour. *What am I doing here? I had almost become a part of the slogan-shouting feminist crowd while the victim awaits justice. I should get out of here right away.* The women's noise faded as she walked away from the crowd. She looked intently at the media van standing next to her. It was an unfamiliar name. She hadn't heard of this news channel. Perhaps they were new and were experimenting with untrained reporters. Pritha took the turn around the corner of the road and headed towards her home, her mind in even deeper chaos.

10

The Curse

Pritha decided to take a bus back to her home, not so much because of the distance as the state of extreme fatigue that she felt. As she boarded a minibus, she heard the loud sound of a radio. The local station was playing the latest film song, and it was blaring from the bus' stereo system. Soon, the bus was full of people and it zoomed out of the station. Out on the main road, it raced tall among a crowd of cars, like a six-foot adult running along with a crowd of toddlers. The bus jumped and jerked and tossed on the road and threw the passengers left and right as it took sharp turns.

Pritha, sitting stiffly on one of the aisle seats, clutched the handlebar in front of her with one hand, and with the other, balanced her bag on her lap. *Why was the driver driving this way?* The thought immediately created curiosity in her to see the man's face and the rear-view mirror hanging above the driver showed her just that. No, it was not a criminal's face. The man did not appear to be drunk either. It was an innocent, calm face, a face that was composed. The expression on his face announced, 'This is the only way in which a bus should be driven'. The driver apparently thought it essential to drive the giant vehicle in this manner.

Pritha looked around at the other passengers on the bus. Some were clutching their bags, some their seats, and many of them the handles of the seats in the front. All of them had calm faces that seemed to say in unison, 'This is the only way in which the bus should be driven'. Pritha's eyes went back to the image in the mirror: a perfectly serene face with ruffled, curly hair. Curly hair! The traumatized face, with pleading eyes, had curly hair.

The song playing on the radio ended and a news capsule began. The first headline caught everyone's attention and murmurs started floating in the bus. The mayor of the town had died after a cardiac arrest a couple of hours ago. The driver slowed down the bus, perhaps unconsciously. Pritha could see almost everyone saying something or the other to their co-passengers. The middle-aged man sitting behind Pritha said to her companion, 'For sure, a curse has fallen on the city. The mayor did not have a history of any disease. He was my brother's neighbour. He was a healthy man. This is the curse of the deity. Temple rules should never be broken.'

Another voice came from behind, 'The sinner himself did not die. Does everyone hear? The sinner is still alive. That means other people must share in his burden. More people will have to pay for the sin. Had he died, the story would have ended.'

A woman sitting a few seats ahead of Pritha displayed a translucent polythene bag to the women around her. The bag had some colourful things but the most prominent were the coconuts that it contained. 'I have bought the necessary things to purify my home. Sisters, you all must get these things too. Save yourself from the curse.' The ladies around her got instantaneously interested and started asking questions about what all things were to be bought, in which quantity and how the ritual should be performed.

'Make a note,' the lady announced. 'You must request one of the temple priests to perform these rituals for you. That is the best way to do it. The head priest told this to me personally.'

Pritha felt sweat on her palms again. She wanted to stand up in that bus and announce the truth, to shout on top of her voice that God had not punished that poor curly-haired man; other men had committed a crime against the poor man. Pritha clenched her fists and controlled her urge to speak out. She closed her eyes and visualized herself telling the truth to all these people. She saw frowns that soon turned into frightful gazes. In an instant, she saw herself running down a hill with the people and the priests following at great speed, hatchets in hand. They were shouting for her head; they wanted to tear her and spill her blood. Her eyes flew open. She took her hanky out of the bag and wiped the sweat off her face and neck.

Pritha felt suffocated; the slimy monster had resurrected and had started peeping through the windows of the bus. She looked out on the other side and saw a fruit-seller behind a cart. A little girl, around five years of age, was tugging at his shirt, apparently asking for something. The bus moved quickly and Pritha lost sight of the man. Perhaps the child wanted food or money or something simple from her father. *What if the man wasn't there? Who would that poor child turn to? What happened to the curly-haired victim's family? A child could become fatherless… just to satisfy some stupid whims of some fake priests?* Pritha sensed herself regaining her strength. The monster had melted and had flown below the bus. *If only Mili had been there by my side, to discuss and to figure out what to do.*

✼

As Pritha rang the doorbell of her house, she saw two large coconuts hanging by red threads on the sides of the main door. On either side of the door, the floor was smeared with a yellow paste, perhaps turmeric. Two pieces of betel nut were placed on one side and a few grains of rice on the other side. As Beena opened the door, Pritha shot her a question, gesturing towards the coconuts and the floor.

'What is this, Ma?'

'Purification. Come in fast. I have other things to do.'

The furniture in the living room had been moved to the sides to make space for the rituals Pritha's mother must have conducted. There was a pattern of a star with some figures marked on the floor. Ants had already started moving in queues to feast on the sugar and the flour with which the pattern had been made. Incense burned at the side of the pattern and emitted soft-perfumed smoke.

'Wait, before you go to your room, take this in your hands,' Beena said urgently, while handing over a mixture of some grains, turmeric, sugar and some unidentifiable powders to Pritha.

'Why?' Pritha asked in irritation.

'Every member of the family has to be purified. Even your aunt and uncle participated in this process before they left.'

'Uncle and aunt left? They were to stay for two more days!' Pritha said in surprise, half-consciously extending her hand to accept what her mother was giving.

'They had to. The priests said that it would be better if people who were not of this town, stayed away from this place. They thought it was better to leave. They'll come sometime in the next month. Don't worry.'

Pritha looked at the greasy mixture on her hand and asked her mother. 'Did you go to the temple today?'

There was satisfaction in Beena's words. 'I and my friends were planning to, but the priests and Guruji have been kind enough to pass on the message to the people. Everyone is now aware of the requirements. Otherwise, it would have taken us half a day to go there and come back. Now, go to the tulsi plant in our backyard, leave this at the root of the plant and pray for forgiveness.'

Pritha hesitated for a second and then looked at her mother's face. In a low voice and heavy breath, she asked, 'Ma, what if no sin was committed?' Beena looked up, startled.

Pritha looked deep into her mother's eyes. 'How do you know

that entering the temple after dark is a sin? What if the man died by…accident or something?' Pritha felt her heart throbbing fast. She was unsure of whether she was going to let the truth be known. Was she ready for this? Was her mother ready for this?

'What, child? What have you been thinking of? Everybody knows it is a sin. The man has offended the deity. Now, don't get into such argument. You are too young for that. As you grow older, you will understand more of the seriousness of religion.'

Pritha could see the rigid faith in her mother's eyes. It was the kind of faith that could not be broken easily. It was faith which was placed in the wrong place and was moving in the wrong direction. Beena touched Pritha on the cheek, 'My child, there are a few things that cannot be questioned because…they cannot be explained in worldly ways. It is best to follow what everyone believes.'

Pritha stood glued to the ground, trying to find out ways to tell the truth to her mother. Just then, her father emerged from his room, office bag in hand. 'Hey Pritha, you are back early? It's good, in a way. I'm leaving for the office. I'm quite late. Alright then, see you both in the evening.' Pritha knew Beena must have detained him to complete the 'purification'.

'Papa…' Pritha followed her father to the main door as Beena went into the kitchen. 'Papa, why is Mummy getting into all this weird stuff? Why does she follow these rituals and superstitions like some old-fashioned, uneducated…?'

Pritha cut her sentence midway as Brij raised his hand, gesturing to her not to speak. He then signalled to her to go to the small front lawn. He shut the door carefully behind him and walked up to the main gate. He placed his office bag on the pavement and his phone in his pocket. Pritha looked at him questioningly and repeated, 'Why is Mummy behaving like that?'

'Child, I can see that you are uncomfortable with what your

mother is doing. I understand that people of your age don't believe in such stuff...'

'It is not about my age, Papa,' Pritha cut her father's speech midway. 'It is about superstition. Ma is getting drawn into weird superstitions.'

'It gives her peace, child. If she gains some peace of mind by going to the temple or by hanging coconuts around her door, there is no harm in that. If your mother thinks it is going to help in some way, she will be at ease.'

Pritha got even more impatient, 'That is not going to help in any way.'

Her father glanced at his watch and replied casually, 'Don't bother yourself with this stuff. Focus on your studies. What your mother is doing is not going to harm anyone. And think of it, she does get peace out of her faith.'

Pritha remained silent. It was true that her mother had been in the habit of getting tense about everyday affairs. She could take stress to a level after which, she would fall ill with high blood pressure or a fever. Of late, she had calmed down. Pritha looked at her father, 'Papa, should faith be connected to all this weird stuff? Can one put faith in fake things?'

Her father smiled, 'A stone is a stone because you believe it is a stone. A stone can be a healing deity if you believe it has powers.'

Her father's words percolated deep down into Pritha's mind. She stood thinking. Her father did not believe in these stories and the superstitions, yet he was so comfortable with their presence in his life! It was as if a man would allow poison-filled bubbles to fly around him believing they would never burst. Brij patted Pritha on the shoulder and shot out of the gate towards his car parked on the side of the road. Her father's words ringing in her head, Pritha looked at the mixture in her hand. She went to one corner of the small lawn, took a dry twig and dug two handfuls of earth with it. She brushed off the mixture in her hand into the hole, covered it with soil and put a stone on top of it. She thought for a moment, and then pushed the stone downwards with great force.

11

Lonely

Pritha sat alone on a wooden bench in a classroom, staring at the pen in her hand. The class had gotten over and the students had moved out. For the next hour, this room would remain unoccupied. She looked out of the window at the grey clouds that had been gathering in the sky. It would surely rain after some time. Pritha turned her attention to the notebook on her desk. She opened a blank page and started drawing shapes—cloud-like shapes, squares, circles, unrecognizable flowers... She drew something for every thought that crossed her mind, unknowingly. The shapes were soon mangled by crosses and unending curved lines, till they were no more recognizable.

It had been almost two weeks since she had tried to lodge a police complaint. The chaos in her mind had not cleared; there was no way in sight. These past days had been of extreme sickness; she felt as if there was no cure. Apparitions of guilt hovered around her constantly. Food had lost its taste and sleep had lost its peace. She attended classes but did not understand the lectures. She had no one to talk to about her condition. Even if there was someone to talk to, it was no use talking to fearful, apprehensive people, who would doubt her at first, and then avoid her like an infection.

To Pritha, it seemed as if a shadow of fear had fallen upon the town. Even the crowd in her college, comprising of young people and supposedly logical-minded teachers, was scared. Everyone believed that a curse had befallen the town. *For sure a curse has fallen upon this town, the curse of wrong belief. Perhaps, I should forget about it. Life would be normal, like it was before all this happened. Maybe I should let things be as they are.*

Pritha made a brave attempt to normalize her life in her imagination, to bring things back to how they were before the incident, by forgetting that the incident ever happened. She closed her eyes and visualized herself starting an ordinary day, as she did earlier. She was dressed and standing outside her home, ready to go to college. She saw the entire town from that station, as if mounted on a live canvas. She started to walk but could not move around; there was no spot on the ground where she could step... blood oozed out from the earth; the soil was maroon with dried blood, yet spurts of fresh blood burst out from places. Skeletons limped around the town, gaping at her through the empty sockets of their skulls. The only healthy people were the priests, standing on high pedestals, flashing whips made of flowers. Pritha could see the rusty iron strings of the whips concealed by flowers. A massive apparition, larger than the town, floated in the sky. It was the image of the victim's face...pleading eyes encased in a rim of curly hair. The eyes had a stony gaze that rested upon Pritha. The apparition wobbled with the air, but the eyes fixed their gaze upon her. Pritha shuddered and opened her eyes. She wiped the sweat off her hands and forehead.

Then she repeated to herself the thoughts that had been churning in her mind for the last few days, thoughts that had tired her out so much that she was now afraid of thinking.

I am the only one who knows the truth, but I am one whom no one would believe. I have to do something... I have to ensure justice. Else, this...this...will haunt the town, will haunt me, will haunt the universe eternally! Pritha looked around and tried to breathe easy. *That won't be easy. I wish someone could help me with this, or at least share my burden!*

What can I do? She tapped her pen on the table. The sound resounded through the room. She looked out of the window again. Students moved about on the college grounds. She had seen Mili in the morning. *Why did she not attend this class? Is Pankaj present in the college? Would they be together again?* She saw the swaying trees and the rustling bushes as wind started to blow, announcing the anticipated arrival of rain. The open windows swayed with the wind. A whiff of air entered the room and brought with it the mild fragrance of jasmine flowers. Pritha turned her eyes to the garden to see where the jasmine plants were.

Through the corner of her eye, she saw the tall figure of Rohan entering the room. She kept looking out of the window, pretending not to notice him. She wondered why he had entered the classroom where she was alone. She assumed he must have forgotten something and must have come back looking for it. She got a little alarmed when she saw Rohan was moving in the direction of her seat. She expected him to stop and look around the desks. He did not stop. And Pritha saw his figure walking straight up to her. Her heart throbbed unusually.

'Hi,' Rohan said with a slight smile.

'Hello,' Pritha looked at him.

Rohan looked around, as if trying to decide where to sit and finally sat down on a bench opposite Pritha's seat, ensuring he maintained a respectable distance. He put his bag on the desk in front of him and began in a soft tone, 'I wanted to talk to you about something. Do you have a couple of minutes?'

Pritha immediately put up a deterrent. 'If it is about Mili, I don't need to discuss any of her affairs with you.'

'Of course! I never meant to get into any of the personal matters concerning your friend. Now, if you want me to give a clarification, I can.' Rohan spoke with such eagerness that made it obvious he wanted to present a clarification, whether it was asked for or not.

Pritha looked at him without saying anything. He continued, 'I knew of Pankaj's intentions. I also knew of Mili's belief in a person she should not have put her faith in. Mili is a good girl and I thought if I can do something to save her from harm, I should do it. That's why I spoke to Vandana and—'

Pritha cut in crisply, 'I've already thanked you for that help.'

Rohan fell silent and looked at the floor. He fiddled with the phone in his hand for a while and then steadied his hands. A minute passed in silence and then he said, 'If you can spare a few minutes, I want to talk to you about something that is not related to other people.'

Pritha blurted out a spontaneous response she had not expected from herself, 'Listen, you are friendly with everyone in this college; please be. You might be of great help to the people around; it's your choice. Other people…if they think they have a friend in you, I don't care. I, for sure, have nothing to do with you.' Pritha swallowed hard, surprised at her own reaction. *What is it that I am trying to protect myself from?*

Rohan leaned a bit forward, apparently unaffected by her onslaught. He said in a warm, velvety tone, 'Why do you always stay on your guard, Pritha? You always have this "I can manage on my own" kind of thing around you.'

Something melted inside Pritha at the tone of his voice; something took the shape of a fluid, ready to burst out through her being. She opened her bag and threw the pen and the notebook into it, gulping down a lump in her throat. She closed the zipper of the bag, put the bag on her lap and moved to the edge of the chair, making it obvious she wanted to leave. Yet she thought she should answer him. 'Why are you concerned about my attitude?' she asked.

Rohan leaned backwards and threw his hands up in the air, speaking earnestly, 'Why don't you let other people help you? We are classmates after all. Why do you stay so distant from everybody?' After a slight pause, he added in a soft, caring voice, 'Is there anything I can help you with, anything I can do for you?'

Startled, Pritha looked at him sharply. She quickly turned her eyes away, afraid that they might reveal something to him. Her eyes flitted around the room for a couple of seconds and then she glanced at the crowd that could be seen through the window. Trying to bring confidence back into her eyes, she looked again at Rohan. He looked silently at her. Pritha gazed at the floor. Thoughts rushed past like a whirlwind in her mind. *How pleasant would it be to have someone who cared, who might find a solution for me, who might take all the troubles out of my life!*

She was dumbfounded with her own thoughts. The imagined feeling of having a caring company was so seductive that she let it linger on in her mind. Rohan looked around at the empty classroom and suddenly realized this was not a perfect setting. Alarmed, he spoke hastily, 'Look, don't get me wrong. It is nothing of this "I like you" kind o' thing. Uh…you know…it is nothing of that stuff. Perhaps, I should have spoken to you somewhere else. I hope you don't mind that I came in here. It's only that I thought we can share our problems.' He took a pause and added more calmly, 'See, I respect you and just thought that I might help you in some way. You have been looking kind o' sad for a few days.'

'Thanks!' Pritha said casually. 'I have other work to do. I'll have to go.'

Rohan widened his eyes in helplessness. He got up and made way for her. She looked at Rohan's face as she went by him. There was a look of disappointment, or perhaps hurt on his face. She felt her heart throbbing fast; she knew not why. Her voice softened as she said, 'Bye.' Rohan nodded and looked down at the floor.

Pritha walked towards the exit of the room. Something inside her wanted her to stay, to sit down and to simply look at Rohan. The desire grew stronger as she neared the door. For a moment, she thought she would turn and run back to him; she thought she won't care a damn about the world and would hold him in her arms and cry on his shoulder. She would cry her heart out, sharing her anxiety, her fears with him. Yet, she walked mechanically towards the exit. She found an extraordinary passion taking control of her, something very different from usual; something that coaxed her to rebel against her own nature; something that wanted her to let go of her loneliness and to run into Rohan's arms.

She approached the door when two boys whom she recognized as her classmates entered the doorway. One of them was a friend of Rohan. He saw Pritha, and in a flash, his eyes searched for the other person in the room, Rohan. A dirty smile lined his jaw just as he suggestively winked at his companion. Any other day, Pritha would have taken him on for the crime of misinterpreting. That moment, she just walked out into the corridor.

Her heart beating faster, she took heavy steps along the corridor. It was a long one, lined with rooms on one side and flanked by the lawn on the other side. Rain had begun to pour generously, and students who were on the lawn were running back indoors. She did not make any effort to look around for familiar faces. The momentary passion was rapidly transforming back into a desire to stay alone. It was impossible to stay alone, however.

'Hey Pritha!' a sharp voice called out from behind. She turned back and saw a group of girls and boys of her class approaching. Beyond them, she could see Rohan coming out of the classroom, looking sombre.

'Should we add your name to the list? Are you in for the IP?' One of the girls put a straight question at Pritha. She recalled that this group had been working hard towards organizing an

'Introductory Party', a ritual at this college that took place at the beginning of every session.

'Yeah, I'll be coming.'

A girl wrote Pritha's name on a printout they were carrying and spoke while she did that, 'We have decided on the dress code: saree for girls and Indian ethnic for boys; time is 5 p.m. Is Mili coming? Haven't seen her for a couple of days,' she added casually.

Pritha diverted the discussion, 'We don't have a colour code, do we?'

'Nah. Anything!'

Pritha smiled, gestured a 'thumbs up' and left the group behind.

12

Love?

The college gardens twinkled with decorative lights that night. The DJ played popular music and the voices and cheering of people rose up from the otherwise drab mountainside. The arrangements for the gathering were spread over two different levels of the gardens, connected by a flight of stairs. The party had been going on for over an hour but Pritha had not interacted much with anybody. She did not know why she was here. She did not know much of why she was doing particular things these days. She could not stay at a place for too long, not even in her room. The loneliness at home was getting increasingly suffocating. What she had not imagined was that false smiles at a social gathering could be equally stifling. She sat alone at a table on the far end of the lower lawns and looked at the white pearl bracelet on her left wrist.

From a distance, Rohan looked at Pritha. Her shapely figure lent gracious beauty to the purple crepe-silk saree she was wearing. He noticed the string of pearls around her neck, the white pearl earrings peeping out of her shiny, straight hair and the light make-up on her face. He started walking towards her. Unaware of this, Pritha was turning her bracelet around her wrist when she heard Rohan's greeting. She looked up and her thoughts ran into the events of the previous day. A rush of strange emotion bathed Pritha. Was it something she was feeling for this guy? Was it something else?

Rohan said casually, 'Everyone's going up there. You seemed to be in deep thought…you didn't notice this lawn is almost empty, so I just walked up…' He paused and looked at her.

She said mechanically, 'Yeah. We must go up there.' She stood up, hesitated for a brief moment and went up to stand beside Rohan. The two started walking together. Upstairs, the stage performances began and the music got louder. Yet, the two experienced a succulent silence around them. Confusing thoughts took flight as they walked. A whiff of breeze bought with it the scent of unseen emotions. Pritha's arm gently brushed past Rohan's arm as she raised her hand to adjust her hair. The pleats of her saree waved in the breeze and touched his legs.

Pritha didn't look up to see his reaction. She was aware of her attractiveness that day. She knew if she just looked at Rohan with that tiny curve of a smile, and that shine in her eyes, a story would begin. She knew he was watching her constantly. In that semi-darkness, with the dim glow of the distant lights falling on her face, the pale pink colour of her lips and the black shimmer of her eyes seemed to be the only things full of life.

Pritha gave full freedom to her imagination. It would be nice, yes, pleasant, to have somebody who cared. She imagined the squeeze of someone's hand on her hand, someone's caress in the hair, a hug that would take her troubles away. The two reached the staircase. Not used to wearing a saree, she hesitated before taking the first step. She gathered the pleats with a gentle clasp of the fingers of her right hand. In sudden spontaneity, Rohan offered her his hand. Pritha looked up at him. He tilted his head in request. She smiled and slipped her left hand into his. They began climbing up the flight of stairs as the music got louder.

He is holding my hand…we are walking close together…

The two climbed up a couple of stairs, almost wishing that time would slow down. Rohan glanced at Pritha. She looked at him. This time, she paid attention to his eyes. Something was out of sync, something in those eyes was in disharmony with her being. She consciously observed how his skin felt on her hand. There was a deep, subtle difference between their microcosmic vibrations, which she could feel but could not comprehend. At the midway landing of the stairway, she started paying attention to her thoughts. She observed that Rohan was smiling broadly now, but was amazed at what she herself was feeling. *I am perfectly comfortable! There is no shiver in my body, no shine in my eyes...no blush on my cheeks. We are walking so close together. There is no one around. Yet, I don't feel anything!*

A revelation struck Pritha and she felt herself coming out of a trance. She had no idea what Rohan wanted, but she could see herself clearly, as if her inner core had been revealed to her. She felt a gentle stroke of comfort in her mind, the kind that comes from clarity of thought.

No, he is not the one! I can do perfectly well without him. It won't make a difference to me if he vanished from the planet right now.

As they were about to reach the top of the staircase, Pritha left Rohan's hand and said a bland 'Thank you.' He smiled and kept looking at her. After a minute of silence, he said, 'You are looking beautiful...!'

Pritha cut in before he could finish his sentence, 'Don't get me wrong, Rohan, but I think we should be happy just being classmates. I mean, we can't be friends...or more.'

The colour drained from Rohan's face. He stood lifelessly. Pritha added, 'It is just that I have so many things in my life that I want to avoid a few other things. Just that.' She did not know the meaning of her words and she didn't know what to say, but one thing she knew was that the time to halt was now. Rohan managed to find some words, 'Yeah...Yeah... Of course.'

He struggled to find more words. Pritha looked on, hoping she had not been the cause of hurt. Yet, she did not feel apologetic.

Confidence in her decision brimmed through her countenance. She saw Rohan's face changing colour. He uttered in a small voice, 'I just wanted to be of help. I feel you are in some kind of trouble. Can I do something about it?'

Pritha shot a startled look at him, taken by surprise at the relevance of those words. *Does he know something about it? No, that's not possible. But then, why do I have the feeling that he does know something?*

She muttered, 'I'm fine. Everything is fine.' Then she looked around and added, 'I think your friends are waiting for you.'

Rohan gave a blank look in the direction that she had pointed. With an unconcealed expression of sadness, he moved towards them. She looked around for a vacant seat and proceeded to the one most distant from the stage. She sat down, the weight of loneliness weighing even more heavily upon her now. She looked around at the lawn full of partying people. Suddenly, the people seemed to fade. A clear, stark image of a curly-haired man rose like a phantom from behind the hill. Pritha gaped at the image in front of her eyes as her breathing became shallow and her hands became sweaty.

∽

The next morning, Pritha reached the college early. As it had been for the past few days, she wanted to flit around impatiently all the time. There was still twenty minutes to the class when she entered the campus. To avoid meeting anyone, she headed towards the cafeteria. She entered the hall and looked around for a table. *How come there are so many people here this morning? They must be bunking in celebration.* There was only one unoccupied table, the one where Rohan sat next to her a few days ago. *This is silly humour. Coincidence has contrived this situation!* She went to the counter, ordered tea and proceeded towards the table. After hesitating for a moment, she sat down at the seat where Rohan had been sitting the other day. A battle of thoughts rocked inside her head.

What is all this that's happening to me? What if I had actually gone back to Rohan in the classroom the other day? What if I had given him ideas last evening? Goodness! Am I going crazy? Why did he come up to me? He mentioned 'help'. Why? What does he want to help me with? Does he know anything about...that...that incident? Not possible.

Cranky shit! I should give my mind a break. What am I thinking of? He was only behaving like a concerned acquaintance, nothing more. But why is he concerned about me? It is plain that he gives a lot of attention to me. There was something special in his eyes last night. No. These boys are all alike. They use the tool of sympathy to sway girls...girls, who don't use their minds. Gosh! Why do I, of all the people on earth, crave for support? I definitely can manage things on my own. She tried to give a lot of thought to the last point. *Is it wrong if I try to manage things on my own?* A familiar voice startled her as it interrupted her thoughts.

'What an awful, repelling shirt this is, the one you are wearing.'

Pritha gave a quick look at the lemon-yellow half-sleeved linen shirt she was wearing. It was a gift from Mili. Pritha loved the shirt and wore it on days when she could not decide what to wear. Pritha turned her eyes back at the speaker. Mili stood with her arms folded, looking at Pritha's shirt. Their eyes met. Pritha waited in anticipation. Mili waited for Pritha to say something. The two fumbled for words. Pritha spoke up.

She pointed a finger at Mili's face, 'Your eyeliner is smudged.'

Mili let out a tiny gasp and quickly took out a paper-wipe from her bag. She handed it over to Pritha and sat down by her side. Pritha carefully wiped out the extra kohl around Mili's eyes and gave back the wipe to her. She gestured at the canteen boy to come to the table. 'Bring one more tea, please.'

The two girls sat in silence, a silence that was a medium to express such myriad expressions as cannot be expressed in words. That quiet togetherness was like a magician's act that could repair wounds, cuts, bruises of the mind. The two girls' hearts were filled with such relief that they avoided talking. They sat sipping tea, hardly looking at each other, afraid of words. Their hearts were full of regained happiness. Words would only undo that.

13

The Eyes

The next afternoon, after the classes got over, Pritha found herself reluctantly treading up the road to the mountaintop temple, with Mili by her side. The previous day's silence had begun to melt, giving way to words. Mili had been doing most of the talking. Pritha was glad because she would have struggled to speak like her usual self. Besides, she knew Mili desperately needed to share what she had gone through, to maintain the sanity of her mind. Pritha listened patiently as they walked up the road. Mili had convinced Pritha to accompany her to the temple, a suggestion that Pritha had outrightly rejected at first. After refusing to accompany her friend, she had suddenly realized that in the deep recesses of her mind, she too had a hidden, inexplicable desire to go up there, at least once again. Mili anyway, would not listen to a 'no' and the two were here, progressing up the hill. She could not say 'no' to Mili but could not say a 'yes' to herself either. That place was the root of all her suffering, it was at this place that everything had started, after which her life had become a mangled mass. Nothing remained the same.

Mili described how she had been depressed, hardly coming out of her home and not taking any phone calls for the last few days. Soon she realized that she should not 'make herself suffer because of an unworthy person'. She wanted to lead a normal life once again. Pritha watched Mili as the latter talked passionately about every thought, every feeling she had experienced. She tried to see deeper into Mili. *Should I tell her about the incident? Would she believe me? Would she support me? Can she suggest a way out? Hardly, I guess...like the other people, she has faith in this place. But I do really want to go up there once again. What is this thing that is causing me so much of uneasiness?* Pritha looked around as she recognized a familiar sensation in her mind; she looked around for the invisible monster. It was not there. *I'm not a coward hiding inside my own mind! It's just that there is no way I could bring justice to that man.* Pritha looked up at the sky. *Somebody, help me, please! Show me a way!*

'Mili, are you sure you really want to go to the temple?'

'What's wrong with you Pritha? We are almost there. It means a lot to me. Ever since I was a child, I have been coming here. This place gives me peace of mind and you know that,' Mili said, surprised at Pritha's question. Pritha nodded as Mili continued, 'I've been doing things that were not, uh...um...quite right. I must go to the temple to kind of...thank God...for saving me from trouble...by...by sending a friend at just the right time.' She looked at Pritha and added, 'But you dare not feel proud of yourself!'

Pritha smiled. Inwardly, she wondered how visiting that place would help Mili get rid of her guilt. Mili kept on talking, while every minute, Pritha weighed the option of confiding in her friend. They were near the temple gates by now. Pritha looked up to see a koel that was singing up on a tree close to the gate. Her eyes fell on something that looked like a piece of plastic. *Closed-circuit cameras! CCTVs in the temple! They keep a watch on who comes here and goes out! Can they record in the dark too? Yes, this area was pretty dark that night. Perhaps, the street lamp was not functioning.* Pritha felt anxious. She wanted to take Mili by the hand, to run down the road, to run away from that place and to tell her about her ordeal. Walking in that state of turmoil, she did not realize that they had entered the main hall of the temple. Pritha looked around, dazed. She pressed her forehead to ease the pain that had started, when she realized her palms were sweating. She looked around the hall.

There were around a dozen people waiting in a queue to make offerings to the deity. As always, there was a priest between the idol and the people, who moved along the demarcation of the steel railing. Mili signalled to Pritha and they went to a corner of the hall, the farthest distance from the idol. Mili sat down on the floor and joined her hands on her lap. She closed her eyes and seemed to be meditating. Pritha sat down beside her silently. A thousand voices rang inside her head, drowning the sounds of the hall. She closed her eyes. The only vision she could see was that of the curly-haired man lying helplessly on the floor. His muffled sounds became louder until they started hurting the insides of her head. She saw the vision of a girl peeking through a window at the man, the girl who had seen it all, and done nothing, the girl who had come here once again to sit on the floor where the man had been reduced to a sack. Sweat trickled down from Pritha's forehead onto her arms. The pain in her forehead grew. A thousand sounds grew into a million. Pritha's lungs felt choked. She suddenly opened her eyes, realizing that she was breathing heavily, very heavily.

Pritha took out her hanky with quivering hands and wiped off the sweat from her face. She opened the lid of her tumbler and took a sip of water. She then looked at her friend; the latter's eyes were still closed. She wondered what peace she could draw from a place like this. There were only two people left in the queue. She looked further at the priest who was mechanically tossing various offerings at the table placed at the foot of the idol. Like a machine, he dumped prasad onto the hands of the people. Pritha looked beyond him, at the idol. The form of the idol had been concealed with shiny clothes and numerous garlands. But there were the eyes that were not hidden. There were the eyes that did not blink, even for a second. *These eyes must be watching everything, must have been watching everything.* Pritha looked into those eyes; the distance was no barrier; she made eye contact. *Those eyes did see everything, and the owner of the eyes did nothing. Yet, I don't feel any anger towards the owner of those eyes. Why? Those eyes watched...and my eyes watched too.* At this, sensation radiated from her spine. *Only that pair of eyes besides mine saw what happened here.* Pritha looked at those eyes, unblinking, from that distance. She was mesmerized. She wanted that moment to go on, forever.

The priest had attended to the people in the hall and now looked impatiently at the two girls sitting in the far corner of the hall. He waited for a few seconds and thinking that the girls would take time, took out his phone and dialed a number. In the process, he left his place and walked towards the exit of the hall. He was soon out in the garden, engaged in a conversation. That was a perfect setting. Pritha felt a magnetic pull, asking her to approach the altar. She tapped on Mili's shoulder and moved ahead. Mili opened her eyes and followed Pritha. Mili looked around to see where the priest was. It was customary to wait for him before offering anything at the temple.

Pritha walked towards the altar, still looking at those eyes. Both girls reached the steel railing separating the visitor's area from the idol and folded their hands. Pritha made a lucid movement around the railing, closer to the idol. A shocked Mili whispered, 'That's not allowed, Pritha. Come back!' Pritha ignored her friend's words and went straight to the idol. She lowered her eyes. An intense desire took over her to touch the God of that temple, to feel Him and to feel His energy. With her hands, she cleared the flower petals from the base of the statue and touched the stone. Her hands on the stone were gently shaking while her mind experienced a deep calm. She wasn't aware of the tears rolling down her cheeks.

'Come back, Pritha. You should not be doing this! It's only the priest...' Mili panicked. Pritha ignored her words and did not move her hands, her face flooding with tears. Mili turned back to see if the priest was back. He was still out in the garden on his phone. A few seconds later, Pritha turned around with a smile and joined her friend on the other side of the steel railing.

'What were you doing?' Mili scolded her friend. Then she noticed the tears. 'Are you okay?' she softened.

'Never better.' Pritha made no attempt to wipe off the tears. The tears had made her aware of being alive, like a life-potion. She turned around and said, 'Let's go. I have lots of important stuff to do.'

'But the prasad? We can't leave without taking that...'

'I've already got it, Mili,' Pritha said in a voice laden with pure bliss.

Mili was confused but she was also used to the occasional strange behaviour of her friend. She waited for the priest. The latter came and dumped prasad onto Mili's palm. By then, Pritha had stepped out of the hall, smiling. She looked around. The leaves of the trees were the eyes, the petals of the flowers were the eyes, the black ants on the earth were the eyes, and the birds in the sky were the eyes. *No temple can imprison those eyes. I can touch anything on this planet and can share the bliss. It is available!* Mili caught up with Pritha and offered her some of the sweets on her palm.

There is no need for it, Mili. There never was. The prasad cannot be imprisoned in a tiny bit of sweet, my dear. It is all around us. But that would confuse Mili too much, so she took what Mili offered. The two girls started towards the town, one having gained peace after an action, and another having gained peace in the necessity of acting upon something. As they walked down the road, Pritha paused by a huge rock on the roadside, weathered by the rain and the winds. Smiling, she looked at it and touched it with her hands.

She closed her eyes and chuckled with happiness.

An even more confused Mili asked, 'What are you doing now?'

'Connecting to the network; the signal's strong.' Pritha smiled broadly. 'Mili, you go to the college and attend classes. I'll have to go somewhere else,' Pritha said resolutely.

Exasperated, Mili grasped Pritha's arm, forcing her to stop from walking. 'What's going on, Pritha? Something's not right.'

'Give me some time, Mili. I will share things with you; I have to.'

'Fine! Then I'll come with you.'

'You can't,' Pritha said decisively. 'Just have a little more patience with me. Please…'

There was something in Pritha's tone that made Mili let her go. She tried to fight off her confusion and decided to wait. After Mili left, Pritha progressed towards the bakery on Circle Road, the place where these extraordinary events had begun.

14

Hope

The corridors of the office of the superintendent of police weren't crowded during the morning hours. A few people moved around with serene faces. Pritha sat waiting on a bench, impatiently scrolling up and down on her phone. Taking an appointment with the SP had been difficult, since the office clerk was not used to a student walking in wanting to have a conversation with the police chief. He was rather used to handling people with criminal complaints or people who at least appeared harassed or capable of harassing others. He had granted the appointment with a warning, 'You will have five minutes. Sir is a very busy man.'

Pritha recalled the events of the previous day. She tried to comprehend what she had experienced at the temple, outside the temple and everywhere. It was beyond words. It was as if every cell in her being had been reprogrammed towards calmness. And with this state of fearlessness, she could see a path of action. Helplessness had been transformed into a powerful desire to do something, without fearing the result of that action.

After sending off Mili to college, she had gone to the bakery on Circle Road, got the name and address of the victim and had visited Victory Colony. The meeting with Babulal's wife had shaken her, yet it had infused a steely resolve in her to fight for truth. She thought of the poor couple's dwelling, of the wooden face of the man, of his wife, and wondered how their children might be coping.

After waiting for a good twenty minutes, Pritha was shown into the office of the SP. The latter was a man in his early forties, with shades of grey in his hair. His smart appearance and sincere eyes put Pritha at ease immediately. She did not waste much time in narrating what she had witnessed at the temple on that night. The officer listened to her attentively, patiently. After hesitating initially, she also narrated her experience at the police station.

'Sir, the thing is that I do not know what to do to bring justice to this man. Yet, I feel I must do something about this. What happened to the man was criminal. His life and the lives of his wife and children have been cruelly torn apart. Nobody in the town knows that the paralyzed man is a victim, not a sinner. I thought you should be the best person to turn to. I can't even share this with my parents because if I do, they won't let me go out of the house. They would force me to keep quiet, fearing for my safety.'

She looked at the officer in anticipation. The SP remained silent, deep in thought. Pritha started getting nervous. *Have I come to the wrong place? Is he another believer of the temple's way? Does he think I am playing kiddies' pranks? Does he believe me at all?* The officer leaned forward in his chair and stared at the register in front of him. Pritha maintained an anxious silence. At last, the silence was broken.

'What's your name, kid?'

'Pritha, Sir.'

'Pritha, do you know my name?'

Pritha shook her head, a little embarrassed for not having done that much homework.

'My name is Yusuf Jamal.'

She stared at the officer in total confusion, trying to locate that name in her memory. The officer continued, 'I have served in this profession for more than twenty years. I have often been posted at sensitive locations. I have gunned down terrorists; I have faced bullets and grenades for the people of our country.' He took a pause and his tone changed. 'Yet, if I lead a police team to conduct an investigation on the temple, leave alone a raid, I will be called a Pakistani.'

Dead silence filled the room for a few seconds. Pritha was at a total loss for words. The pages of a register on the officer's desk fluttered in the air coming through the window. Then she blurted out, 'Sir, that man has been wronged. This town is engulfed in wrong belief. I really don't know what I can do. But I have to do something.'

The officer looked keenly at Pritha. 'You know, kid, when it is a question of right and wrong, I would go out and blast it. I don't care a damn about what people would say. However, you are talking of a temple tradition that is perhaps a few decades old. Things like this don't just affect individuals. They have the potential of burning out entire cities. We live in a confusing world where the illusion of faith is more important than real faith.'

Disappointment was written large on Pritha's face. The officer leaned back in his chair and thought for another minute. 'I'll ensure that he gets medical treatment. I'll speak to the hospital staff.' Next, he picked up the phone and dialed a number. He directed the person on the other end to ensure that he registers a complaint by a student named Pritha when she comes up to the police station. The authority in his tone was unmistakable. He disconnected the call and explained, 'I can see determination in you, Pritha. In the current circumstances, the best course is the way of the law. The first thing is to register a complaint since you are a witness. Go to the police station that falls in the temple area. I have directed them to file the report. Let me see what I can do to chase the case after that.'

Pritha felt some relief. She got up and thanked the officer. As she neared the door, the officer called, 'Do you have some proof of that assault, a recording, a video or something?'

'No...' Pritha got thinking. 'Sir, only if the man himself can speak... but he does not seem to be in a condition to utter even a word.'

'Hmm. Let's see. Go ahead.'

༄

Pritha felt relieved that she had come to a different police station this time. The complaint was registered, though while writing it down, the officer appeared shocked beyond explanation. Twice, it appeared to Pritha that he wanted to put down his pen and to ask Pritha to get out of that place. Perhaps, he thought Pritha was hallucinating. After all, he was a local man, a man of this town. Despite that, he had to follow the directions of the superintendent of police.

Having filed the report, Pritha came out of the police station hastily. It was getting late and she needed to get back home in a hurry. The uneasiness, the anger and the frustration inside her, which had been her companions since that evening, seemed to have taken some rest. There was some minor satisfaction that gave her energy. Mili, however, had to be told about all of this. She could not be kept waiting for too long.

15

Warning!

'Have you ever seen how milk curdles? I mean, how milk matures into curd when heated to a higher temperature and a spoonful of curd is dropped into it?' Pritha posed the question to Mili, as the two walked towards the college together the next morning. Mili looked at Pritha with unconcealed annoyance. Pritha had not been answering the string of questions she had been putting to her. Rather, she was talking about curd. Mili was intensely concerned about her friend's unusual behaviour and had begun to feel that there were quite a few things that were not right. A minute ago, Mili had demanded that Pritha tell her the reasons for her strange behaviour. In response, Pritha had shot this stupid question at her. Mili lost her patience.

'I have no interest in cooking, Pritha. Just come to the point.'

Pritha continued, her patience exasperating Mili, 'You must have seen how hard corn beautifully transforms into popcorn when heated?'

'Enough of this nonsense! You have been behaving so weirdly for the last two days and now this crap…What's wrong with you?' Mili shouted. She grabbed Pritha's hand and pulled her to the rain shelter on the side of the road. The two sat with their backs to the valley. There was no one on the concrete benches of the shelter at this time of the day. 'We are not going a step further, you hear? Not a step further, until you tell me what's going on.'

Pritha peered into Mili's eyes and uttered softly, 'I have been through an inferno, Mili. The heat has been too much. But now, I've started to find a way out.' She looked at her friend's confused face, took a deep breath and narrated the incidents since that evening at the temple. She sketched every event, every thought, every emotion that she had felt. Her throat ran dry but she didn't take a break. She passionately told her friend how her life had undergone a drastic change in the last few days.

She finished her narration and looked into Mili's eyes. The latter looked back as if she was looking at a stranger. Pritha had expected her to be shocked, but it hurt her to see disbelief in Mili's eyes. *Doesn't she believe me? No, it must be disbelief at the events. She trusts me, of course. Maybe she is too shocked.*

People on the road went by and glanced at the two girls sitting in silence. Mili fiddled weakly with the strap of her bag. Pritha gave her time. A good five minutes passed in silence and then Mili stood up and spoke sharply, 'Pritha, get back home as fast as you can. Don't leave your home for a few days. I have a feeling you might get into some sort of trouble. And most importantly, what do you think you are? What do you want to become, a national heroine? Why did you lodge a report? Don't you understand these are religious matters? They are beyond our understanding. Listen to me and forget all about this. Go home and be a normal girl.' Mili was breathless.

Pritha looked at Mili rather calmly and said, 'Let's go.'

Mili followed reluctantly. Pritha led her friend not towards home, but the college. Mili did most of the talking and tried ceaselessly to persuade Pritha to go home and forget about the incident. Pritha could sense fear in her friend's words. She observed how Mili was unconsciously keeping some distance from her. She wondered if Mili was feeling uncomfortable in her company. She thought how strange it was that the contrast between their states of mind was increasing. The more fearful Mili felt, the stronger became the resolve in Pritha's mind. *Strange, but I don't feel any fear.*

The girls reached a lonely stretch of the road. This area had a rocky hill on one side and a deep valley on the other. There weren't any buildings around because of the particular topography of this small area of the town. To build anything on that rocky slope or on the landslide-prone valley was unthinkable. So, this stretch of around half a kilometre remained wild, with just the road passing through it. Some cacti dangled from odd patches on the rocky side of the hill. As the girls neared a narrow curve on the road, a car with tinted glasses almost brushed past them and stopped a few metres ahead. The girls shrieked faintly. The driver's door opened and Rohan walked out. He waved at the girls as he walked towards them. Mili cried with relief, 'Oh God, you scared us!'

'Sorry! I am not an expert driver. That is a borrowed car.' He laughed, trying to sound friendly. 'Do you mind taking a lift from a friend with a borrowed car?'

Before Mili could say anything, Pritha cut in, 'Thanks Rohan, but we are feeling good walking down the road.'

'Come on, I won't kidnap you! We are going the same way.'

Pritha said sharply, 'Isn't your insistence getting a bit weird? We are not even friends.'

'But we are classmates. I can offer you a lift for that reason.'

'Don't detain us, Rohan. We have to move,' Pritha said firmly and asked Mili to move.

The shine in Rohan's eyes faded. He glanced at the car. A rear door of the car opened and a man in a white dhoti and a saffron kurta emerged. It was the head priest of the temple. Mili squeezed Pritha's hand as her heart began pounding with apprehension. Pritha shot a glance towards Rohan. He avoided her eyes and his face went pale. Pritha remembered the face of the police officer who had to write down her report. *How his face oozed out dislike for me! He must have called up the priests as soon as I left.* The priest walked towards the group and glared at Rohan. 'Boy, you are useless! Your grandfather and your father have served the temple so well, but you are a good-for-nothing fellow! Your father will be disappointed he sent you to help us!'

Rohan's face got clouded with the dullest shade of grey just as the priest looked at Pritha. Mili, pale with fear and anxiety, squeezed and held Pritha's hand tightly. The priest began in a tone of urgency, as if he did not want to waste time dealing with introductory remarks.

'Girl, we know that you have been taking too much of an interest in the matters of the temple. You have also taken upon yourself a sin, a grave sin, by meeting the sinner. I don't want to drag this. Let me tell you straightforwardly…' He pointed his index finger at Pritha, 'Don't interfere in divine matters. You will be destroyed!'

Pritha looked deep into his eyes. She felt amused at what she saw. There was impatience in those eyes; there was discontentment. As if by contrast, she felt a sea of energy rising within her. In a calm voice, she said, 'You are right! No human being should interfere in divine matters. Human life is a divine gift. Of course, we can be destroyed! What if right now there is an earthquake and this mountain crumbles upon you; or standing here, you are struck by lightning? Or, what if that insect on your shirt was carrying a deadly virus that had been sent to infect you?' The priest panicked and shrugged off the insect in disgust. Mili, aghast at what Pritha was doing, let go of her hand in shock. Rohan looked up at her, startled. Pritha kept looking at the priest and made no effort to contain a tiny smile that escaped from the corner of her lips. She could see the priest getting infuriated. *Was it so easy to unsettle him?*

The priest stepped closer to Pritha and said threateningly, 'I am giving you good advice. Stay away from the matters of the temple. There are things you do not understand.'

Pritha said calmly, 'Please explain the things I do not understand.'

The priest made a futile attempt to control his anger and unwittingly shouted, 'You are a knowledge-less human being. Temples are high institutions that have to maintain rules, rules for the populace to remain obedient. There are things that religious institutions have to do for the larger good of humanity. We have to teach the common man to follow the path of religion and at times, we teach them through punishment. It is not an easy task to keep a whole population on the religious path. Temples are divine places and the rules of such places cannot be challenged by low mortals like you.'

Pritha listened patiently to every word the priest said. Then after a pause, she said in a low, firm voice, 'Sir, how many times have you felt the presence of the divine? Had you tasted the spiritual manna even for a microsecond, you would have freed yourself from the bondage of rules. You would have realized there is no such thing as a low mortal. Look at that ant crawling on the ground. Perhaps, the life of that insect is more precious than yours!' Pritha was surprised at her own words. *Perhaps there is a design… I now know things that I perhaps did not understand before. Have I got access to a tiny portion of the treasure of the universe?*

The priest snorted heavily in rage. Pritha continued, 'The temple is not a high institution. It was not created by God; it was created by human beings, by you. You are the ones who set the rules; God did not.'

Perspiration dotted the priest's forehead as he clenched his fists. He growled, 'You fool! It is God who directs priests to set the rules for temples.'

A terrified Mili pressed Pritha's hand, signalling her to stop the conversation.

Pritha ignored her friend and cut in sharply, 'Yeah, in a dream does He direct? What if tomorrow I have a dream that I should go up there and destroy your temple? That would be God's directive too, no?'

'Enough of your sinful impudence!' the priest thundered. 'You don't know the kind of powers that I have. You will vanish and no one will get to know where you have gone—'

Pritha interrupted the priest midway, 'Listen to me.' There was a mysterious calmness in her voice. The priest paused unwillingly and looked wide-eyed at her, perplexed with the calmness in this young girl's voice. Here was a girl who was not intimidated either by his power or his warning. The serenity of her countenance shocked him. This girl was talking to her as a mother would talk to a child. Pritha continued gently, 'I don't think it's your fault that you are following the rules of the temple. You are merely walking on the path shown to you. But please, for a moment, think for yourself. If God does exist, can you confine Him to that temple? Can you ask Him to stay inside the temple premises? Can you decide who has proximity to Him? Listen very carefully, sir. If there is something called God, logically, he must have looked at you every moment of your life, he must have known all your secrets.'

The priest stood rooted to his place in silence, struggling to find words, struggling with his thoughts. After a few seconds, his eyes fluttered and he looked down at the road. He narrowed his eyes and said to Pritha, 'You will pay a price for this'. The thunder in his voice was replaced with shaky words.

He walked back towards the car. Rohan jogged after him and they drove off. Mili's face was pale with terror and her eyes wet with tears. 'Pritha, what are you doing? Don't you know how dangerous all this is? These are powerful people. Oh God! I am so scared.'

Pritha held Mili's hand comfortingly, 'Don't utter the words "God" and "fear" together. That's a bad combination.'

Mili looked wide-eyed at Pritha and shrieked, 'You are going crazy! They can do anything to you, Pritha!'

Pritha thought for a moment and then quietly said, 'You are right, Mili. I'll have to ensure they cannot do it. I have to skip college today, too. I'm going somewhere else. You wanna attend classes?'

'I'm feeling queasy, Pritha. I'll go back home.'

After seeing off Mili, Pritha hastened her steps and walked towards Ganj Bazaar.

16

Unsafe!

Pritha sat across the reporter's desk in a small cubicle at a regional newspaper's office in Ganj Bazaar. The reporter, a woman around thirty years of age, was typing at her laptop—'finishing off a story', as she had told Pritha. She had asked Pritha to wait. The latter sat quietly and observed. She couldn't help but notice how the reporter's eyes looked inverted, since only the lower eyelid had been lined thickly with black kohl, leaving the upper eyelid almost nude. The most striking thing about the reporter though, was the embroidery pattern on the neckline of her beige cotton kurta. The pattern, made in herringbone stitch, was in red and dark brown colours and from a distance, it gave the appearance of human skulls mounted on long bones. Oversized black metal earrings dangled from her ears. Her brownish-black wavy hair had been loosely tied into a bun with a wooden clip. Pritha knew that though the reporter was not looking up from her screen, she was keeping an eye on her, as she was in the range of sight. Perhaps she was not taking her seriously, thinking that she must be here for some petty college issues. Fifteen minutes passed by.

The reporter closed her laptop at last and looked questioningly at Pritha. In the next few minutes, Pritha had summarized what she had seen at the temple, how she had lodged a report and how the priest had threatened her. She expressed a desire to get the information published in the newspaper. She thought that once the news was made public, her safety from the temple people would be ensured. Her parents would be shocked, but she would brief them beforehand.

'So, ma'am, would you be publishing this in tomorrow morning's newspaper?' Pritha asked with some hesitation.

The reporter raised her eyebrows, 'What you have told me is simply shocking. No one would believe this story. The people you are naming are the most respected people of this town. I'll have to do some hard work on it.'

Pritha eagerly added, 'I don't mind if you use the word "allegation", I mean that I am alleging this incident happened.' She looked expectantly at the reporter.

The latter narrowed her eyes, twisted her lips in sarcasm and said, 'Girl, do you think journalism is like your college essay-writing? This is real, dangerous stuff. It requires guts and most of all, a great amount of talent.'

Pritha remained quiet. Despite her inexperience in worldly affairs, she could easily diagnose the vain pride that the reporter suffered from, or it could just have been a feeling of inferiority about working at a local newspaper rather than the big names around. Pritha wondered where the offices of the big newspapers in the town would be. Perhaps, it would be too difficult to get to them, she thought. This was a local paper and they were more likely to print her story. As Pritha sat thinking, the reporter said, 'I will have to verify the facts. That requires a lot of fieldwork. More importantly, I'll have to talk to my editor as well.'

Pritha pondered on how that event could be verified. She thought of mentioning one helpful piece of information. 'You can see the victim's condition for yourself, ma'am. That would be good proof. Maybe with treatment he can speak. I know his address. He lives in—'

'He is dead,' the reporter cut in. 'The man who was found at the temple died this morning. This is this morning's breaking news!' The reporter gave her a look of authority as if pitying a non-journalistic creature for her lack of breaking news.

Pritha sat glued to her chair. *He died? Does anyone ever die of paralysis?*

'How? I mean, why…' Pritha managed to utter feeble words.

The reporter leaned forwards and said, 'Well, the superintendent of police pressurized the civil hospital to admit that man. And look at this: He died within half an hour of being admitted. It would be mighty interesting to see what the temple priests say about this.' Then raising her eyebrows, she said, 'The role of the SP is itself questionable. The town will want to question him.' Pritha knew by the 'town', the reporter meant the 'media'.

She thought for a moment and added, 'Well, though your story seems unbelievable, it has spice in it. Hmm…I'll have to do some work with it.'

Pritha wanted to pose a question but the reporter got up from her seat and opened the jute handbag on her desk. She sifted through the stuff inside for a good amount time before she gave Pritha a look that said, 'When will you get out?' That made Pritha uneasy and she stood up. The reporter was visibly relieved at this and said, 'I'll get back to you by this evening after having a word with my editor. Meanwhile, let's investigate the death of the sinner.'

Pritha felt discomfort creeping into the air around her. She felt a sudden need to get back to her home. She left her mobile number with the reporter and walked out of the newspaper office.

The walk to her home included crossing around half a kilometre through the narrow Ganj Bazaar. The road had shops on either side. This part of the town was always crowded and when one walked through it, one was sure to bump into someone known, the unavoidable side-effect of living in a small town. Pritha noticed that the bazaar was decked up with paper flags and glittery decorations hanging by long strings. The decoration ran along the length of the street, forming a colourful, perforated ceiling. The sound of an approaching loudspeaker echoed in the bazaar. Two boys carrying a microphone-set on a bicycle were announcing the time for the jhanki or the carriage-procession the next day. It was an annual celebration in which the priests of the mountaintop temple took out a procession through the town. The reason behind this ritual was not known, but for the townspeople, this was a local, religious festival and the attendance was enormous. The procession was taken out in the month of August, when the Mahaguru had seen the 'vision in his dream'. The day was decided by the temple priests and the public was let known. On the day of the procession, the presiding priest, along with his associates, travelled on a carriage along the main roads of the town, chanting and showering blessings on the people. *Oh, it is monsoon…time for the procession. I had almost forgotten…*

One could hardly walk speedily on this street. The road was narrow, the shop displays had extended out onto the road and there were people moving in both directions. So, Pritha tried to negotiate her way through the crowd as fast as the circumstances allowed her to. Her mind flitted from one thought to another. She thought of the best way to tell her parents about everything, but there was no best way. There was only one way—just tell them.

Her thoughts flitted to Rohan. That score had to be settled. Anger towards him quickly gave way to relief, strangely. Pritha closed her eyes for a microsecond, even as she walked. She felt relieved that she had not given in to her impulse that day. *What if I had actually turned back and ran into his arms? What if he had put his arms around me…uhhh…yuck! I was saved! Was he always working with the priests?*

Her thoughts were interrupted as her eyes fell on a shabbily dressed boy sitting beside an array of statues displayed along a makeshift roadside shop. He could not have been more than ten years old, but he seemed to be perfectly at ease with the art of selling idols. He called out to people, trying to attract their attention to his merchandise. Pritha paused and looked at him. The little boy looked at her. As their eyes met, Pritha saw immense calm residing in them, as if a whole ocean had become tranquil. She stepped closer and knelt beside the display of idols. She looked at the smiling boy and wondered if she had noticed his presence in this market earlier. She asked, 'Don't you go to school?'

The boy replied, 'I will, as soon as I have finished my work. Buy a statue, madam. It will bring good luck to you. These statues have been made from special clay taken from the riverbed. See this one.' He picked up a green and red idol of a goddess and displayed it to Pritha in his outstretched hands.

Pritha's eyes, however, had already been hooked to a yellow and white idol with clearly defined black eyes. She picked up the shining idol with both her hands and looked at those inanimate eyes. The boy smiled and set the one in his hands back on the mat, looking at the customer who seemed to like the piece she had picked.

While the boy wrapped the purchase in a newspaper and tied it with a string, Pritha gave a nervous look around; to check if any of her classmates or other acquaintances had seen her buying this 'religious' stuff. The boy handed over the package to her and smiled. 'Good luck, madam,' he said. Pritha held the packet in both her hands and stood up, carefully holding it close to her body. She walked away, dazed with the illogical nature of her own action. For once, she did not want to reason out with herself. She had done something that her rational mind couldn't imagine, but her soul mysteriously craved for, at least at that moment.

∞

Pritha raised her hand to ring the doorbell when she heard the sound of unlatching from inside. The door opened and Mili stepped out, followed by Beena.

'Mili?' Pritha's tone instantly conveyed her annoyance as well as numerous unasked questions to her friend.

Mili looked at her friend and could make out that she understood her purpose of coming here. She immediately defended herself, 'I had to do it, Pritha. Sorry, but I did it for your safety.' Mili walked away just as Pritha shot a look at her mother. There could not have been a more evident expression of a dark—awfully dark—fear on that face. Beena grabbed Pritha's hand and pulled her inside with a jerk. She locked the door behind her and double-checked that it could not be opened. As Pritha stood there in the living room, Beena went to every room and with shaking hands, latched each door and window, including those of the kitchen and the washrooms. After checking each entry to the house, she dropped down on the sofa and started sobbing.

In between her sobs, she muttered, 'Oh, Amu, we are damned! We are damned! What have you got yourself into? Why did you become a part of a sin? Hadn't I told you about the temple? We are damned!'

Pritha kept the package and her bag gently on the dining table and went into the kitchen as her mother's anxiety-laden voice followed her. She came back with a glass of water and gave it to her mother. She sat down on the sofa opposite and watched a red-eyed Beena take small sips of water from the glass. The doorbell rang. Her mother's eyes widened in anticipation. Pritha noticed the same but went to the door and peeped through the keyhole. It was her father. He came inside quickly, threw his bag at the table and touched Pritha's cheek lightly. Then he rushed to Beena's side. He held her in his arms as the latter started crying, even more tearfully.

'Maa?' Pritha shouted in reprimand, 'Why are you crying? Please, first try and understand what I am going to tell you.'

Pritha's tone shocked Beena. Pritha had never spoken to her parents like this. That paused her crying. She looked at her daughter, surprised.

Pritha sat down on the sofa opposite her parents. 'Look, Ma, Papa, I know this must have shocked you. But please understand that in the first place, I went to the hilltop that evening to save Mili's life. She was…distressed and I feared she might take her own life!' Her parents gave a curious look at Pritha, but the latter did not want to get into the details of that discussion now. 'Second, and most important, I witnessed an injustice; I witnessed the shattering of a myth; I witnessed the wiping out of a poor man's life. What you and all the people around this town had believed was untrue. The God in that temple is not interested in taking anybody's life for trespassing; only the priests do that. I saw that with my eyes. Do you think I should have kept quiet about this? If I did, that would have been a sin for sure!'

Pritha paused and looked at her parents. Beena was so overwhelmed with anguish that she would repel any logical argument. Brij didn't care about the priests, but he was anxious for his wife and his daughter. Pritha went closer to her parents and wiped her mother's tears with her hands. She stood with her hands on her mother's shoulders.

'Look at me, Ma. Just think, why was I the only witness to that incident? Don't you think it was kind of planned…by God or somebody? Why was I there at that very moment, witnessing that incident? Maybe, the God you have been worshipping for so long wants to get something done through me. See, it has been so many days but I am safe.' Beena looked up at Pritha as the latter added, 'See, I am safe. No harm has happened to me in the last few days.'

Pritha's words startled Beena. She got calmer and looked down at the floor, deep in thought. Brij smiled at his daughter and conveyed with a gesture that he thought Pritha had managed to soothe Beena, at least temporarily. However, what could await them was too scary to be imagined.

17

Lonely, But Not Alone

Caravans of dark grey clouds travelled by the town that afternoon, not really wanting to shed their moisture, but only casting their shadows. Pritha entered her room, clasping the idol she had bought that morning. The newspaper wrapping still cuddled the clay figure. Pritha's father was trying to call up some contacts he had in the police service while Beena had fallen asleep in her room, worn out with exhaustion. Pritha's parents had decided that till the time they got some police protection, none of them would leave the house. In her room, Pritha saw her cluttered study table that had no space for an extra thing on it. With one hand, she pulled aside her wooden study chair and placed it against the wall. She put the package on it. She stood up and looked around when she was startled with the ringing of her phone. She grabbed it and received the call before the sound escaped her room. It was the reporter calling.

'Hello,' Pritha said, her voice laden with expectation.

'Hi Pritha, I am calling you about the story you told us this morning.'

'Oh yes,' Pritha said eagerly.

'Listen, our editor found your story interesting. We are considering putting it in tomorrow morning's edition. Your life is in danger, right? I know you are a student, but can you talk to your parents and tell me how much can you arrange?'

Pritha stood on the floor like a concrete pillar. She could not understand; she was not even sure she clearly heard what the reporter had said. 'I didn't get you, ma'am. Could you repeat what you said?' The reporter said patiently, 'I said, how much can you arrange?'

Confused, Pritha asked, 'Do you charge a fee?'

The reporter laughed as if one might laugh at a monkey trying to use a cell phone. Then she began in a grave voice, 'You are levelling an extremely serious and damaging allegation against the most revered people of this town, and you don't even know how things work out in the practical world? Listen, the temple people are ready to pay us more than forty lakhs. Can you give us a better deal?'

Pritha held the mobile phone more firmly. Her palms were getting sweaty and slippery. Her heartbeat was almost audible to her ears and her breathing got quicker. On the other side of the phone, the reporter found it hard to bear the eight-second silence that followed.

'Hello?' she said impatiently.

Pritha gave herself another couple of seconds and began in a voice full of resolution. 'Yes, of course, I can give you a better deal.'

'You can?' The reporter shrieked in surprise.

'I'll tell you about the amount a bit later, but first, listen to what I have to say. As a student, as a young person, I had always held the media in high esteem. I believed you support the right cause in every circumstance. Today, I came to know what exactly you and your league are doing. You are the kind of people who would spray poison inside a dormitory at night and in the morning, you would pretend to be saviours carrying people on stretchers, shouting at the "apathy" of the people around.'

The reporter intervened, 'What nonsense—'

Pritha cut her short, 'Let me finish. You will hear me out.

You know what price I can pay you? It is peace of mind. It is not something that your forty lakhs could buy for you. You are a decomposing piece, a stinking human. No, you are rotten! And you make the media stink too!'

At this, Pritha cut off the call and threw her mobile phone on the bed. Her eyelashes did not make any attempt to hamper the tears flowing out of her eyes. Her last hope had been murdered. She sank down on the floor and placed her head on the chair. The vision of Babulal's twisted body floated before her eyes. His muffled sounds at the temple seemed to fill the air around her. She closed her eyes but tears continued to flow. She let the tears flow down her face, making no effort to wipe it off. This had been Pritha's little secret, to have short bouts of crying when she needed the most strength. Every time she cried in disappointment, somehow, the tears carried away all the undesirable thoughts from her body, leaving behind a fresh and determined mind. She let the sadness flow out.

∽

It was eleven in the night. Pritha's parents had retired to their room. It had been a mad day. Her father had spent the day calling up the people he trusted, checking if any of them could find out ways to keep the family safe. The police might be siding with the temple and they couldn't really be trusted. Her mother had spent most of the time with her chin resting on her hands, muttering outbursts of disbelief and distress.

In her room, Pritha paced around. It was hard for her to believe that there was no way in sight. Deep inside, she still had faith that there must be some way, some way of staying safe, and more importantly, of telling the truth to the world. She stood up and went to the window. She looked out at the dark sky, trying to locate the moon. It was not to be seen. She came out to the backyard, silently closing the door behind her. As she had done numerous times, she sneaked out towards her secret heaven. This night though, the moon wasn't there, not even a sliver of it, or maybe it had already strolled past earlier in the evening. She sat on her rock and looked up at the sky. Countless stars made the clear sky look glittery. So many times, in the past, she had sat near this rock, sometimes on it, and enjoyed the company of the king of the night sky. Why was it hiding today? Pritha had a craving for the moon's company, to soothe her mind as these meetings had done many times earlier. The glittery sky stared back at her, perhaps disinterested, perhaps in wholehearted support. Pritha looked up.

O You, stars and the moon,
Companions of my loneliness,
I have watched you many times, watching me,
And saying nothing.
Why do you watch me so,
And say nothing?

Moments of silence passed. The cool breeze carried with it loads of freshness, as it had done unfailingly forever. It touched Pritha in a gentle caress. She gathered her arms around herself, acknowledging the touch of the breeze. But she was cross at the moon, for not being visible. She looked at her house. How anxiety filled up that place today, but out here, she did not feel any fear, any anxiety. She was out in the open, unsafe according to logic, but safe in the realms of her mind. Once again, like a caring parent trying to appease an angry child, the breeze hugged Pritha. Her countenance changed.

Well, what difference does it make? At the greatest depths, you, air, are the same as that moon out there. Invisible is not the same as non-existent. It is perhaps the night of the new moon... Startled at her own thoughts, Pritha closed her eyes. *I cannot see the moon, but it is out there somewhere. Perhaps it has sent a message to me through the breeze. Why did I buy that idol...? The message...! I got it!*

Pritha got up and hastened towards her house. *Invisible is not the same as non-existent. There are ways, there are solutions, there definitely are ways...*

She entered her room and looked around. The idol lay on the chair, still wrapped in newspaper. The black print on the paper ran in all directions, difficult to read from some angles. Pritha crossed her legs, sat on the floor and started to peel the covering. She rolled the pieces of paper in a bundle and tossed it to one corner of the room. She sat on the floor, looking at the yellow and white figure that lay calmly in front of her. Then she looked into those eyes. Minutes of stillness went by, each moment soothing Pritha's senses. A sudden gush of emotion overpowered her, such as she had never experienced before. She touched the feet of the idol with her fingertips and gazed at the image. Clay and flesh formed a strange bond and sent up spirals of reassurance in the air. A rhythm vibrated in Pritha's mind:

*No way in sight, but I am not lost.
No one with me, but I am not lonely.*

She looked in adoration at the idol, as if looking at a friend she had been waiting for a long time. Her thoughts cleared and she felt a sea of resolution bathing her. *Let tomorrow morning come...* she whispered to herself.

She then opened her cupboard and dug through the pile of clothes on the lowest shelf. She took out a few pieces, checked them out and folded them back again. After a lot of sifting and turning, she found the pieces she had been looking for. She closed the cupboard and placed the pieces carefully on the bed.

Brij opened his eyes at eight in the morning, when bright sunlight invaded his bedroom. He glanced at Beena, sleeping with her forehead tied with a scarf, her way to manage a headache. The two had stayed awake almost the whole night, having slept only around five in the morning. Brij had been repeatedly telling his shaken wife 'nothing bad is going to happen'. Every time he uttered those words, he wondered how powerful the temple gang would be. Would they think of causing any harm to Pritha? As he got up from his bed, out of habit, he looked at his phone and checked the messages. His eyes got wider as he read a text message from Pritha, sent around an hour ago.

'Pa, promise me that you won't worry. I had to go out for some time, but I'll be back, safe, trust me. I will be safe. I have locked the front door of the house. Please use the spare keys to unlock if you need to.'

Brij hurried out of the room, noiselessly closed the bedroom door behind him and ran to Pritha's room. She was not there. He dialed Pritha's number and anxiously waited for the call to connect. It didn't. She had switched off her phone. He searched his phone to see if he had any of her friends' numbers. He paced around, tossing around various thoughts in his mind. Half an hour later, a message from Pritha popped up. It said, 'I'll keep updating you about my safety. Please give me at least two hours.' Brij immediately dialed Pritha's number again, but the phone was switched off again. He sank back on the sofa, clasping his phone tightly. His daughter was in danger, but he didn't know where she had gone.

18

The Truth

The main road of the town throbbed with the sound of drums and the clanking of cymbals. A crowd of more than a thousand people inched ahead, surrounding a gold-coloured carriage pulled by two horses. The sequin-decorated garments and the tiaras of the horses glistened in the morning sunshine. The head priest of the hilltop temple sat atop the chariot and periodically dipped a mango twig into a vessel and sprinkled water onto the crowd. Two priests walked ahead of the carriage, singing and chanting, taking turns on a microphone. Drummers dressed in white clothes walked at either side of the chariot. The crowd swelled as the procession moved along the town. Journalists from local television channels and newspapers moved along the procession. The cable operators and the news channels had been telecasting this event live for many years. They moved along the procession, trying to capture the expressions of fervor and devotion on the faces of the people. This was their big event, when viewership was at the maximum. Everyone in this town wanted to be seen on television.

A little distance behind the chariot, Pritha walked among a group of women who were clapping to the beats of the drums and were chanting after the priests. The white salwar and kurta she wore made her look no different from the women around her. She had wrapped a printed stole around her head that partly concealed her face. She held the yellow and white idol close to her chest with its face towards the crowd. She smiled when people folded their hands with reverence as they saw it. Occasionally, she had to pause to let the people bow down before the idol or to touch its feet in reverence. This was the festival day for the town and any image of God would be revered more than it would have been on other days.

The procession thus moved along for half an hour and paused at the main square of the town. This was the place where the carriage would halt for a few minutes, as it was a reasonably spacious part of the town. It could hold a huge gathering as the roads were unusually wide and there were small, squarish parks between the buildings on all the four sides, so people had space to stand and watch the procession. Those who did not or could not walk along with the procession made it a point to at least stand here to have a good look. A giant screen had been installed on a balcony of the second floor of the deputy commissioner's office. The screen displayed live images from the festivities. At this place, when the procession halted, the singing grew louder and the temple people danced as if frenzied by devotion. Children came forward and sang and recited impromptu into the microphone. As this went on, Pritha struggled her way forward through the crowd, coming to the right side of the chariot, close to the priest with the microphone. She waited, her hands clasping the idol tightly.

The priests on foot signalled to the musicians. The drums went silent and the clanking of cymbals stopped. There were only soft murmurs around. Newspersons came closer to the chariot with the aim of covering every bit of this episode of the local festival. Pritha saw herself on the giant screen and stepped back, away from the focus of the cameras. The head priest sitting on the chariot nodded to one of the priests on foot, apparently some kind of a leader in the temple hierarchy. The latter took the microphone and began his speech, 'Glory to the gods! Glory to the temple! May our Mahaguru's blessings be upon us!' The crowd repeated after his words. He raised his hands to quieten the crowd and continued, 'With the blessings of our Mahaguru, this auspicious day has arrived again for this town. May our faith get stronger!' The other priests on foot chanted in unison, 'Glory to the temple! Glory to the Mahaguru!' The leader continued again, 'The auspicious day has come, but this year, people of this town, you are extremely fortunate that you were saved…there could have been a catastrophe. The town would have been wiped out, all because of a man's sin. Our Guru saved us! Glory to the Guru!'

This time the people fell silent. The priest had mentioned the event that had terrified the people. Shadows of discomfort could be seen in the crowd. The head priest sensed this discomfort and he couldn't check the sly smile that escaped the corner of his lips. The man with the microphone gave this ominous silence its two minutes before he began shouting again, 'Jai Mahaguru! Glory to the temple! We were saved, townspeople, we were saved! You have nothing to worry about. The guardians of this town are with you.' At this, the crowd cheered and repeated, 'Jai Mahaguru! Jai Mahaguru!'

The priest gestured to two school children standing nearby. They came closer and he handed over the microphone to them. 'Say, Jai Mahaguru! Glory to the temple!' The children repeated after him. Two more people came forward and shouted, 'Jai ho!' into the microphone. An elderly woman who had been waiting, took the microphone and sang a few lines of a popular devotional song. Pritha had pulled the stole closer to her face and had acquired a position just behind the woman, before a queue could start forming. When the woman finished her singing, she looked behind her, wanting to pass on the microphone to the next willing citizen. Pritha shifted the idol to her left hand and with her right hand, took the microphone from the woman.

'Jai ho!' she chanted emphatically. 'Glory be to truth!' Then she distanced herself a little from the priests, taking the microphone along and quickly added, 'Honourable devotees of this town, on this auspicious day, we have been blessed. Please pay attention to this idol in my hands.' She raised the idol a bit. There were charged murmurs and people tried to look in her direction, finding a line of sight above shoulders and between rows of people. The priests looked at her, trying to figure out what this girl was trying to say.

She added, 'There has been a miracle. God has inspired me. He came to me in the form of this statue and my life changed. All this happened on this auspicious day.'

The priests on foot enthusiastically raised their hands and goaded the crowd to chant 'Jai ho'. The people remained more or less quiet. They were more interested in what Pritha had to say. There was silence again and all eyes questioned her.

Pritha continued, 'Everyone, please mark it, I am going to tell you a miraculous truth, but it is truth laden with danger. If anyone tries to harm me, he would be harming God, whose inspirational representation is here, in my hands. So, don't step forward towards me.' The crowd became silent like never before. The media people came even closer and focused their cameras on Pritha.

She began, 'My fellow people, please listen carefully. I am telling you only the truth. The man who died at the temple…he was not a sinner. There was no curse. He was killed by these temple priests. I saw it with my own eyes. You all have been fooled for too long. God doesn't want to stop you from going into the temple after dark. These priests have created this fallacy. I can't be lying with a figure of God in my hands. If I do so, I'll be blasted this second. Wake up people, as God has awakened me.' At this, Pritha threw the microphone on the road with full force to break it.

The priests surrounding the chariot lunged in her direction, violently waving their hands. One of them reached out to an inner pocket of his kurta and took out a gun. Another priest cupped the pistol in his hands and rebuked the man, 'Keep it inside! Don't take it out here!' The head priest sprung up from his seat on the chariot and shouted, 'That is a lie! That is a lie! Sinner! Grave sinner!'

19

The Challenge

The faces of the priests took on various shades of grey. A few of them ran to the rear of the chariot, away from the crowd. The more aggressive ones moved threateningly towards Pritha, but their progress was hampered by a group of charged-up media persons who surrounded Pritha in no time, complete with their cameras rolling and microphones ready. Pritha had been encased in a protective human shield. There were deafening sounds all around, people were talking in their highest pitch to each other. In this commotion, Pritha quickly dialed her father's number. He received the call immediately, 'Where are you, child? What are these sounds? Come home!' Pritha shouted into the phone to make herself heard in the sea of mixed sounds, 'Papa, I am fine. See me on the live news on the local TV channel. Will talk to you later.'

The head priest looked on from his high station, dazed. He tried to raise his voice to say something convincing to the crowd, but no one looked at him. People looked only in Pritha's direction. Waves of people had started moving towards her. Perspiration bathed the head priest and he looked on like a scarecrow standing amidst a flock of insolent birds who hardly cared for his presence. One of the cameras caught the head priest tumbling down the chariot and signalling to his people. They came together in a huddle and the group disappeared behind the chariot. The camera turned towards Pritha.

The journalists and the local cable TV camerapersons hurled questions at Pritha. They asked in numerous different ways if she had actually said that the temple priests had attacked the man. The questions were incessant and simultaneous. Pritha raised her voice, 'Please let me answer each question one by one. Please!' The journalists fell silent for a microsecond when two of them spoke together, 'You said the priests attacked the man?'

Pritha answered the question affirmatively, firmly, and began describing the events of that evening in detail. She said that she had gone uphill looking for a friend whom she had had a 'fight' with. Then, in every detail, she mentioned what she witnessed at the temple. From the corner of her eye, she saw a reporter's familiar face with thick kohl under the eyes. The reporter stood at the margin of the group, trying not to make eye contact. Pritha paused in her narration and waved to her, 'Hello, Ma'am! So now, do you want to put this piece in your newspaper for free, or are you looking for a good deal?' The reporter was embarrassed and moved away. Pritha smiled and continued narrating the events to the media.

'Did you file a police complaint?' a reporter shouted.

'Yes, I did, but after a lot of struggle. When I finally managed to do that, I got a death threat from none other than the head priest of the temple. So, mark it, that if I or my family lands into any kind of danger, the temple people would be responsible for it. They will want to see me dead.'

After a lot of questions related to when and where that happened, one of the journalists said emphatically, 'So, you want to say that anyone can go into the temple after dark? It would be safe to do so? That the legend was a lie and it was actually the priests who attacked the man? You want to say that the deity will not be offended if one enters the temple after dark?'

Pritha answered, 'I saw with my eyes that the priests injected something into the man that crippled him. The man died because of that. He was attacked by the priests, not by God.'

A loud, charged voice emerged from beyond the group of journalists, 'Why should we believe you, girl?' The passion in the voice called everyone's attention. People looked in the direction to see an elderly man dressed in the local traditional attire of a kurta-pajama and a khadi half-jacket; he was very much a native of this town. The intensity of his outburst made it clear that he had spent his life believing in the temple legend. He continued with a good amount of disgust in his voice as he walked towards Pritha, 'Why should anyone believe you? You are just a kid, and kids these days think it is fashionable to appear non-religious. What do you understand about holy affairs? Are you trying to mislead this town? You are trying to challenge an old faith? I have seen many youngsters like you. They think they appear smart if they insult religion. You are doing the same thing.' The man's face had turned red with passion and he swayed his arms violently as he spoke.

Pritha looked at him with empathy. She had a hundred thoughts in her mind but she quickly filtered out the ones that she thought might cure people like him of their fallacy. Meanwhile the reporters reframed their questions.

'What do you have to say to that?'

She said, 'I don't know anything about religion. So, there is no question of my making fun of it.' She went closer to the man and looked into his eyes, 'Believe me, Dadu!' The man was taken aback at this term of affection. She had used a term from the local language, which meant 'dear grandfather'. She continued, 'I have nothing for or against the temple. Really! I am only recalling what I saw. And I saw that the priests of that temple attacked a man who later died because of what they had injected into him. Dadu, I don't know anything about God. But if there is something called "God", He knows that I am saying the truth. You see this?' With both her hands, she raised the idol in her hands, higher up for the man to see. The latter was startled and he took a step backwards. A strange blend of reverence, confusion and fear coloured his face. He could not speak any further.

Pritha silently uttered in her mind, 'Sorry, dear friend. I am not using you, but I desperately need your help! I couldn't have done it today without you.' As Pritha turned away from the man, a subtle but powerful thought flowed into her mind. She shivered at the realization, 'My friend, I didn't choose you. You chose me. Maybe, I am glad I'm being used.'

Pritha stood in the centre of the circle formed by the media people. She clasped the idol tightly, made a resolution in her mind and raised her voice for all to hear. 'Please, my fellow townspeople, listen to me carefully. I won't ask you to believe what I said. Rather, please come and check for yourselves. I will spend the whole of this night inside the temple. I invite all of you to join me. Let us see for ourselves. If you want to witness the truth about the temple, consider joining me. I'll reach the temple at five-thirty in the evening, today.' Spontaneously, huge waves of murmurs swept across the crowd. Everyone seemed to be talking to everyone. This girl had not only challenged their faith but was also inviting them to become witnesses to a truth they never wanted to be true.

∞

At Pritha's home, Beena and Brij sat on the sofa, holding each other's hands tightly. They were looking at the TV, trying hard not to blink their eyes. The local cable channel wound up their news piece just as Pritha finished with her call to the people. In less than a minute, Brij and Beena's phones got busy. There were calls from neighbours, friends and colleagues. Most of the people who called Brij expressed apprehension. A number of their neighbours warned Beena that their daughter could be the cause of a disaster.

Someone presaged that Pritha is going to be the cause of doom for the town, and the existence of the town would be wiped out forever. The couple had no comments to give to any of the callers, so they stopped receiving any more calls and waited for Pritha to come back home.

Half an hour later, Pritha was at the dining table at her house, taking huge bites into the sandwiches that Beena had prepared for her. Pritha's phone beeped every few minutes. Classmates, old friends and friends of friends were texting and calling up. A group of young people had created groups on social media, spreading the word, asking people to meet up at the temple in the evening. Pritha was not surprised to see very few people answer in the affirmative. Most of the comments were questions about the time she would be entering the temple. Pritha scrolled down her phone screen as she ate. Beena looked at Brij with wrinkles on her forehead. The latter signalled to her to stay relaxed.

Then there was a call from an unknown number. Pritha thought for a second and received the call.

'Pritha, this is Rohan,' a mild voice came from the other end of the line.

Pritha remained silent. Rohan hesitated for a second but added, 'I wanted to say sorry to you for that day. I couldn't do anything. I was asked to lead him to you, since I knew you. Are you listening, Pritha?'

'Yes. What do you want?'

Rohan spoke with a sparkle in his voice. 'I have always liked you. And what you did today was brave...I have no words. I will join you this evening—'

Pritha cut in emphatically, 'The only person whom I don't want there this evening is you, Rohan.'

Pritha could sense the discomfort on the other end of the phone. She continued, 'A person who cannot stand up for himself can definitely not stand up for a cause. You need time...grow a spine! And please don't come there.' She disconnected the call.

Beena looked apprehensively at Pritha. She could sense she was talking to a boy. She opened her mouth to ask something, but then decided not to. She took a deep breath and looked around. Then she said, 'Baby, do you know why all of us are safe? It is because of him.' She pointed towards the yellow and white idol sitting elegantly among other images of divinity in the little shrine of the house. As soon as Pritha had stepped into the house, Beena had installed that idol in her temple, had burned incense and a lamp in front of it, and had bowed with utmost reverence.

Pritha smiled and walked towards the shrine and stood looking at the idol as one would look thankfully at a friend. Their eyes met. She could see the idol expanding, encompassing the shrine, the room, the house and beyond, touching everything on the planet and becoming everything on the planet. She smiled. *So, infinitely big stuff can be condensed into small things! That's magic, for sure! Friend, some people see you only here, but some can sense you everywhere. Hey, in addition to the other things that I want to thank you for, thank you for saving my mom from insanity.* The faith Beena had discovered in the idol was an antidote to what could have happened to her after the falsifying of the temple myth. Pritha felt like standing there forever. The silent dialogue was interrupted when Beena added in a voice laden with concern, 'My child, is it necessary for you to go up there to the temple this evening? Isn't all this enough? I mean, there might be some risk.'

Brij looked at Beena, alarmed. Pritha turned back and looked at her mother. 'Ma, you just said that He took care of me. Have faith! I have to prove what I claimed. The town needs to see the truth!'

20

To the Temple

As the sun hid behind the blue-hued mountains, Pritha reached the foot of the mountain on which the temple stood. A winding road led up to the temple from here, but this was the road on the opposite side of Circle Road, a second access to the temple. This side of the hill faced the main town. She gave a gasp of surprise as she saw a group of around two hundred people waiting there. She looked around and saw mostly young boys and girls with excited faces. There were loud cheers when Pritha approached the gathering. A realization crept into Pritha's mind; she was being treated as a celebrity! A day ago, she was just another girl. A few strong voices came out from the crowd, 'We want to see the truth, Pritha! We are with you.' A girl, who looked like she was interested more in gaining attention than in lending support, came up to Pritha and said in a loud voice, 'Of course, it is nonsensical that some divine being would deny entry to people when it is dark. Why did we not challenge this before?' An even louder voice shouted from behind her, 'Let us see who attacks us today. The priests are in police custody.'

Pritha got alarmed at the direction in which this evening's effort had the danger of heading. It was not meant to be a show of rebellion. Nor was it meant to be a gathering of spoilt brats waiting for their chance to revolt and get their two days of fame. She couldn't let this event be hijacked by such people. She looked around and saw that she was the centre of attention and most of the people were looking at her. They would listen to what she said, there was every chance they would. She raised both her hands to quieten the crowd. As soon as she spoke, there was a reasonable amount of silence. She said resolutely, 'Please! Please! Don't indulge in any kind of angry behaviour. I want to thank you all for supporting me. We are a team now and we must act sensibly. We are not going to harm anybody or anything for that matter. I need your affirmative answer!'

There was a cheer from the crowd. She wondered if it was more out of the excitement of the occasion than out of agreement. She continued, 'Remember, our only aim is to sit inside the temple tonight. We only want the facts to be out. The truth will be seen by everyone tomorrow morning.' There were murmurs of consent. 'Let's go then.'

People moved aside to let Pritha pass. All waited for her to walk in the lead position. An unprecedented thrill vibrated in Pritha's being in those moments. She felt like the most important person on the planet that day. Automatically, she visualized crowds lifting her like they would honour a leader. She imagined herself standing on a pedestal, looking down at the people she had saved. She looked around to see a huge crowd following her and felt like a phenomenal trailblazer marching to the most important gathering in history. *Well, this is important stuff I am doing. It is courageous stuff. I am special!*

Pritha walked in this trance and the group reached halfway up the road. The road was narrower from here and people had to walk closer. A group of friends walking behind Pritha was engaged in a conversation. They joked and laughed and sometimes gave each other high-fives. A boy chuckled and said, 'So, your wish has been fulfilled. You had been bugging us for the past week.'

Another voice said, 'What wish?'

'Your life was getting boring. You needed entertainment, didn't you? Now you have it, that too, live.'

A third voice added in excitement, 'It's hard to believe! Our little sleepy town is having such an adventure today. And it is real! I swear, it beats all reality shows! There is real danger involved here.'

Pritha's steps got heavier. The conversation she had just overheard threw her out of her stupor. *They are here to have fun! Perhaps they are just enjoying seeing me take on danger, using me as an instrument of entertainment. Do they even care what this whole thing is about?* She considered the folly of the thoughts that had clouded her mind a few minutes ago. *How easy it was to get flown into the sea of vanity. How easy! How difficult it must be keeping one's head when crowds listened to you.* For a minute, she wanted to turn around and talk to the people behind her. She thought for a few moments and moved ahead, more briskly than before. Her task was hers after all, no one else's.

In a few more minutes, she entered the temple premises. The crowd followed her. There were more people in the courtyard of the temple, again, mostly young people. Mili, who had been waiting there, stepped forward from among the crowd and took Pritha to a side, holding her hand, 'Do you really have to do this, Pritha? Isn't it enough that you have spoken about this? What if there actually is some danger inside the temple after dark? See, I do not doubt you, but what if the priests' crime is one thing and the legend about the temple is another thing?'

Pritha put her hand on Mili's shoulder in an assuring way and said, 'Mili, there can be many other places on this planet where divinity wouldn't want humans to intrude. Humans should not be digging unnecessarily into the earth; they shouldn't be invading forests for selfish reasons; they shouldn't be leaving their polluted imprints in the water and air of this planet. I don't know if there is something called a God, but if there is a God, what does that magnificent being care for a man-made building; call it a temple you may.'

Mili looked intently at Pritha's face, the meaning of her words stirring something inside her. Yet, she wanted to save her friend from any kind of trouble. She pleaded, although her words defied the tone of agreement in her voice, 'Just for the sake of safety, Pritha.' Then in a deeper, more concerned voice, she added, 'What if the legend is true?'

Pritha pointed to the entrance of the temple. 'Just go and take a look at the idol in the temple, Mili. Look into those unblinking eyes and feel how the energy is everywhere around you, not just in that idol, not just in this building. You will get your answers.'

Mili said in slight embarrassment, 'I can't do that today, Pritha. I have personal reasons.'

Pritha had kept her calm through that evening, but her friend's words seemed to unsettle her. 'Personal reasons? You mean, your regular biology?' Mili nodded. Pritha said in a stony voice, 'If you think that on certain days you shouldn't be polluting God's domain because you are in a particular biological condition, you would have to get off this planet, my friend. Nay, you have to wipe your existence off this universe.'

A shocked Mili looked at Pritha while the latter walked away. TV reporters had begun fixing their cameras around the temple hall. A couple of cameras were stationed on tripods outside the windows that opened out from the hall. Two of the cameramen had positioned their camera stands on the entrance door. Pritha looked around and saw that more people were joining in. At the outer margins of the crowd, she spotted policemen keeping a watch at the gathering and beyond them, she noticed the figure of the superintendent of police, busy in giving instructions to his men.

The darkness of the night started changing the colour and hue of everything. Pritha walked towards the temple and stood at the entrance. She folded her hands, closed her eyes for a moment and stepped in. At this, the crowd let out a collective, lengthy gasp. She was doing what no one had dared to imagine. Pritha walked straight towards the idol of the deity and bowed. Then she sat down on a durrie on the floor. She looked around and saw the empty hall behind her. The crowd looked on through the ten large windows. At the entrance door, curious onlookers peered over each others' shoulders. A few tried to spot Pritha through the mesh of wires and tripods that the news people had installed. However, no one other than Pritha stepped into the hall.

Pritha looked at the time on her phone. It was seven in the evening. She wondered how she would spend such a lot of time that night, doing nothing. With reluctance, she looked towards the part of the floor that had been haunting her, the spot that had shaken her entire existence. She made sure there were no obvious expressions on her face; the cameras were rolling and numerous eyes were looking at her. Her sight fell on the place where Babulal had crouched, begging for his life, the spot where the attackers had satisfied their egos. She had braced herself for emotional pain, as the thought of that incident had induced in her so many times in the past days.

There was no pain that day, though. A different set of emotions had entered her mind. She sensed an unprecedented feeling of satisfaction surging within her. She turned her face away from the crowds and closed her eyes. There was no more anger, no sign of anxiety. Only deep calm bathed her mind. She opened her eyes and looked around at the walls and at the ceiling of the temple hall. The glow of satisfaction bathed everything. She looked at the eyes of the figure of the deity. *Are those eyes smiling? Did I notice that before? How do artists make such representations?*

21

Believers

An hour and a half had passed by since Pritha had taken a seat inside the temple. By this time, she had paid attention to each detail inside the hall—the colour and texture of the numerous objects on and around the altar, the shape of the beads that hung at the fringes and the frames of the huge windows on both sides of the hall. The media people were on constant watch, expecting a dramatic event any second. They queried people about their opinion and got various ominous responses. Some thought Pritha's head would explode. Others presaged the town would drown in a deluge. Some creative ones thought she would lose her speech or sight. It appeared as if the crowd standing outside was there perhaps only to watch one of that happen.

Often, Pritha could hear the news anchors shouting into the microphones. More often than not, they were repeating the same thing. Sometimes, she turned around to look at the people making loud observations about the action she was taking. She was being judged every second and by every person standing outside. From that distance, she saw angry faces, she saw curious faces, but she remained the only person inside the hall. Every time she heard a comment that mentioned her, she turned her sight to the spot on the floor of the hall. Her longing to expose the truth got even stronger and she sat even more resolutely.

'Come out, you sinner!' some people fumed. Their call was

supported by numerous other voices. 'Come out! Come out! You will be damned, and we will be damned because of you.' The voices got louder and angrier. Soon, it became a chorus. Pritha looked around and turned her gaze back to the floor of the temple hall. There was a loud thud and a large stone, the size of a cricket ball, landed next to Pritha. She withdrew impulsively. One of the glass windows shattered as another piece of stone was hurled. The shards flew all over. Pritha stood against a wall, looking out and wondering what to do. Just then, she saw policemen taking control of the crowd. The shouting quietened down. Pritha moved from her position and saw through the windows. Police personnel were keeping a watch on the people and the latter seemed to be intimidated by them, for the time being at least. She looked around at the floor and saw glittering pieces of glass reflecting various shades of light. She went to the adjoining room. The cameras captured the vacant temple hall, numerous assumptions were made and the crowd looked on with even more concentration. A few minutes later, Pritha came back with a broom in her hand. She started sweeping the floor, collecting all the glass shards into a plastic bag. Having done this, she went to the other room once again and came back after washing her hands. The policemen now stood easy, having by now rounded up the troublemakers.

Pritha came back to her earlier seat, picked up the stone that lay on the floor and went to the entrance of the hall. She held out the stone to the people and said, 'You did not hurl stones at me; you tried to throw your non-acceptance at the truth. And this is going to hurt you the most. The truth will still remain the truth, whether or not you want to accept it.' Curious eyes looked on at her.

She put the stone down in a corner of the hall, moved back to her seat and sat down once again. It was comparatively quiet outside, but she did not feel like looking back at the crowd, so she tried to pay attention to her surroundings. A mouse peeked from behind the altar, and seeing no one close by, noiselessly scampered to the front. Very soon, it noticed Pritha and darted back, with a loose thread from the red altar cloth hooked to one of its legs. By now, out in the open, night had painted every object with its own shades of darkness. The two tubelights in the hall were not sufficient to counter the shadows of night-time. Pritha got up and looked around for switches. She went to the wall panel and one by one, she illuminated all the bulbs, the tubelights and the chandelier. She went back to her seat and sat down cross-legged once again. She hoped the mouse would come out once again. She had enjoyed the look on its face, careful but confident, and she understood that its home was somewhere in this hall only. She wondered how that being was so much at ease at this place, while the people outside had such great fears associated with it. She was falling into deep thought, when she sensed movement and murmurs behind her.

She looked around and saw about fifteen people entering the temple. The media persons re-positioned themselves, determined to cover every angle of this new development. Pritha smiled and nodded to the people. They came forward and one by one, sat down on the durries. After a while, another man entered through the doorway, alone. He was a tall man, around sixty years of age, dressed in perfectly creased grey trousers and a spotless white shirt. When he saw Pritha looking at him, he signalled to her with a gesture of his hand. She got up and walked towards him, intrigued as to why he was calling her.

The man smiled as Pritha approached him. He said, 'Good evening, child!'

Pritha refreshed her memory to recall if she had ever seen that man earlier. She said with hesitation, 'Do I know you, sir?'

'No, you don't know me, but I saw you on TV today. When I heard you resolving to come here in the night, I thought that I must come here too. I am a professor of Indian Studies. I work in another city, but I have an old house here that I keep visiting. I am happy that I am here when this town is undergoing this great change. How could I not be a witness to this?'

Pritha looked on at the man's face. *He is speaking as if he knew a change would come to this town. I don't understand.* The professor looked at Pritha's face, laden with confusion and added, 'Child, during my long career, I have made an attempt to understand and observe patterns of human social thinking. And do you know what have I learnt in this long career?'

Pritha shook her head while her curious eyes looked on.

He said, 'I have seen how we make ourselves prisoners of self-created boundaries. We want to confine everything within those boundaries, everything, including the divinity, which we pretend to revere. Do you know why we create those boundaries? We construct those limitations for ourselves because we look at the world through spectacles that have been smeared with fear, with misunderstanding, with ignorance.' He paused and looked at Pritha as a proud parent would look at his child who had won a competition. He added, 'You must be wondering why I am talking to you about all of this.' He paused for a few moments. Then he took a deep breath and said, 'All my life I had believed that humans have imprisoned themselves in those boundaries forever. But you, just a young person, have shattered at least a layer of that…and shown the path of liberation. I don't know you, but I am proud of you!'

There was such emotion in the man's words that Pritha realized her eyes had become moist. She blinked to hide it. 'I had to do this. Else, I would have suffocated with guilt, the guilt of inaction.' Pritha paused thoughtfully for a few seconds. Her eyes widened with a realization and she blurted, 'Oh no…! No! My guilt would have been my boundary! I would have imprisoned myself in it! I would have looked at life through my own smeared glasses.'

Pritha stood rooted, trying to comprehend the situation, trying to find the relationship between what she could have not done, and the professor's revelation. The professor looked on at her face intently, with patience. A few minutes passed in silence between the two while the other people in the hall talked among themselves, unaware of what the two were discussing. The professor smiled and spoke gently, 'You have removed those smeared glasses, child. You have liberated yourself and this town. You had the courage to do the right thing, so don't imagine what could have happened had you chosen the other path, because people like you could never have chosen inaction.'

Pritha looked at the man, in awe of his observations. He smiled again, 'I can see that you have more questions. I'm a stranger to you, but I might be of some help.'

Pritha looked up and added in a half-whisper, 'You've already answered some questions, sir, but I was also wondering why these people came with me. I mean, with me inside the temple. I don't even know them. Are they not scared like the rest of the town? Have they always thought that the temple legend was a lie?'

The man looked around at the crowd. 'Do you see the faith on their faces? Are any one of them scared?' Pritha turned and looked around at the smiling faces. 'These people are the real believers. When one believes, there are no boundaries; there is only freedom. Sometimes these believers only need someone to lead them on.'

Pritha stared at the man's face for a few seconds, stunned by what he said. Then she looked again at the people sitting on the temple floor. Some rested their backs against the wall, some sat cross-legged, engaged in conversation with their companions. He was right. None of those people seemed afraid. They knew what they were doing. She spotted Mili, too, sitting with her back against a wall. Pritha smiled at her. Mili nodded.

A woman, around forty-five years of age, got up, folded her hands and chanted impromptu in a deep, serene voice, 'Au...uu..mm...' A few people repeated after her. She smiled and chanted the same numerous times. In a few seconds, everyone sitting there chanted with her. The hall filled with a sense of oneness, one sound; and one idea seemed to connect all the people present there. The woman took a pause. She moved to the centre of the gathering, raised her hands and broke into a song. It was a devotional song sung commonly at prayer meetings.

Pritha nodded to the professor and whispered a 'thank you'. Both seated themselves in the crowd. This time, Pritha sat beside Mili, just as the two exchanged smiles. The woman, who was singing, uttered every syllable in intense passion. The crowd joined her in the song, repeating as a chorus after her. Her song came to an end and the people smiled and cheered. Within a few seconds, a young girl stood up and started singing a more contemporary devotional song. The group joined in with even more enthusiasm.

Every time a song ended, another person was ready with a new piece. Those who were not comfortable singing, clapped their hands in harmony with the music. The more enthusiastic got up and danced. The sounds floated like weightless fragrant flowers around the hall.

Soon a group of people went forward and started dancing in front of the altar. Among these was a little child, barely six years of age. He held his grandfather's hand as the two swayed to the songs being sung. Pritha observed these people. They were celebrating, but celebrating what? *It is the night of freedom. For me, it is freedom from guilt, freedom from a burden. What are they freeing themselves from? How keen each one of them seems, impatient to celebrate divinity without restraint! They seem to be at peace. Oh! This is beautiful!*

Pritha absorbed the beauty of those moments, unaware that trouble could strike. The night was not over yet.

22

The Night

Midnight approached, but the town refused to acknowledge the otherwise much-loved sleep. The onlookers outside the hall stayed on even as some of them covered themselves up with blankets and shawls. The frenzy of the singing and the fearlessness of the minds amalgamated to form an invisible manna that rose up from the people and spread around. Gradually, the manna filled the temple hall, till it started pouring out through the windows and the doors and gently enveloped the people standing outside. These indirect participants of the event, too, were touched by the magic. They began humming the songs along with the people inside the temple hall. Soon, they joined in the rhythmic clapping along with singing the songs. A few of them started singing as loudly as those inside.

By now, the walls of the temple hall had melted in the magic of music. The magic was everywhere; there could be no holding it back. There were no boundaries. Around a dozen of the onlookers stepped forward, removed their footwear and started swaying to the music. Soon, they threw their shawls on the floor, formed a circle and joined hands. They danced to the songs and after a while, a few of them started entering the hall.

As they stepped inside, the clapping got more rhythmic and the singing got more feverish. People laughed and smiled and many had tears rolling down their cheeks. Never had they experienced such unbounded feelings. They could connect with every aspect of creation, without the slightest shades of fear. They could express their love, their requests and their pleas to the divine without rituals, without rules. There were no limitations. Only pure love pulsated around them. Pritha watched these people with awe; never before had she seen such intense yet innocent undertakings. People looked so beautiful after they shed off the fear they had been wearing all their lives.

In the garden of the temple, an owl perched on the branches of a huge deodar tree looked in confusion at the temple building. The building vibrated with the rhythm of bliss, but what were these humans celebrating? It was beyond the owl's comprehension that this was the night of a grand festival, the festival of freedom for the humans. It had been witnessing numerous birds, insects, worms and moles enjoying the freedom of entering and leaving the temple hall as and when they wished. Those creatures had always known freedom.

It was an hour past midnight when two men arrived, carrying a huge steel dispenser full of tea, and packets of disposable glasses at the courtyard of the temple. They made their way through the crowd and stood at the door of the temple, holding the dispenser by its strong handles. They gestured to the people inside, asking them to take the refreshment. The people did not know fatigue that night, but the offer from the humble-looking, smiling men, was enticing. Two middle-aged women inside the temple got up and came towards the men. Between them, they decided they would do this task of serving tea to the entire crowd inside the temple. It would be nothing less than prasad, they said. The men put the container down on the floor and handed over the glasses to the women. The latter took their positions beside the container and the men disappeared into the crowd.

Just as the women were about to pour tea into the first tumbler, the lights went out and it got pitch dark. A few people turned on the flashlights on their phones. The singing in the temple did not halt. In the darkness interspersed with a few tiny lights, a group of bats charged in from among the trees. Quite a few of them fiercely collided with the tea dispenser, causing it to tumble over. The lid burst open and the entire contents of the container washed the floor and flowed to the grass in the garden. The power came back in a minute and the bats rallied back into the trees.

A panicky voice rose up from among the people. 'There is froth on the floor! There is froth where the tea fell down!'

People stepped back. Their throats ran dry as they saw the grass in the garden wither like burnt hay. Someone shouted, 'Poison!' Another one shouted to the policemen to catch the two men. A voice came out from a distance, 'She will be killed. She will be killed. No one will live with that sin!' Policemen ran in the direction of the voice. The team of policemen huddled together even as two constables charged downhill. Inside the hall, people went on singing and dancing, unaware of what had happened outside.

Fresh rays of the sun filtered through the branches of the trees and fell onto the temple courtyard. The glow of sunshine from the huge windows lit up the main hall of the temple. There were loud cheers around. People hugged each other and made no effort to control their smiles, which often broke into laughter. Nano particles of happiness floated around in the air, touching everything and every being. The TV reporters now entered the hall, barefoot and screamed into their microphones, covering the result of the event.

In this commotion, from a distance, Mili saw Pritha suddenly slumping to the floor, her face in her hands. She saw her crouching down on the floor, her face still hidden with her hands. Mili rushed towards Pritha. Alarmed, she took Pritha by the shoulders and tried to straighten her body. But Pritha would not move. Mili tried to shake her, desperate to see if her friend was alright. Pritha's shoulders were stiff. After a few anxious moments, Pritha raised one of her hands and signalled to Mili. The latter let go and sank onto the floor, her anxiety-ridden eyes fixed on her friend and her hands wringing nervously with stress. People gathered around the two girls. There were loud murmurs, assumptions, negations, validations. A couple of minutes later, Pritha gently sat up and removed her hands from her face. Her face was washed with tears. She looked up and whispered in a choked voice, 'Thank you'. She then looked at her friend and gave the smile of a lifetime. It was now Mili's turn to break down into tears. She stumbled up to her friend and put her arms tightly around her shoulders.

Made in the USA
Monee, IL
03 May 2026

49438526R00090